PEDIGREE DOGS IN COLOUR

BOOK ONE

HOUNDS

*Official Standards
and
Colour Illustrations*

OTHER TITLES AVAILABLE
OR IN PREPARATION

PEDIGREE DOGS IN COLOUR

BOOK ONE

HOUNDS

Roy Hodrien

Official Standards

*Colour Illustrations by
the Author*

NIMROD PRESS LTD

Dedicated to the memory of
Nan and Charlie

First Published in 1990

Pedigree Dogs in Colour   ISBN 1 85259 094 7

Book One – Hounds   ISBN 1 85259 205 2
Book Two – Gundogs   ISBN 1 85259 206 0
Book Three – Terriers   ISBN 1 85259 207 9
Book Four – Utility Group   ISBN 1 85259 208 7
Book Five – Working Group   ISBN 1 85259 209 5
Book Six – Toy Group   ISBN 1 85259 210 9

NIMROD PRESS LTD
15 The Maltings
Turk Street
Alton, Hants, GU34 1DL

Produced by Jamesway Graphics
Middleton, Manchester

Printed in England

CONTENTS

BOOK THREE – **TERRIERS**

BOOK FOUR – **UTILITY GROUP**

BOOK FIVE – **WORKING GROUP**

BOOK SIX – **TOY GROUP**

ACKNOWLEDGEMENTS

My thanks are offered to all those who assisted with this book. In particular I acknowledge the role of the British Kennel Club who gave permission for the *Official Standards* to be reproduced. The American Club also kindly allowed me to quote from their *Standards* showing the main variations from the British Standards.

ROY HODRIEN

PEDIGREE DOGS IN COLOUR

BOOK ONE

HOUNDS

This is Book One in a volume consisting of six books each dealing with a main group of dogs. The page numbering follows that used in the main volume.

Afghan Hound
Basenji

AFGHAN HOUND

It is not difficult to see why this breed has so many devotees. An Afghan in full show condition is often breathtaking.

The history of the breed is fogged in conflicting reports and ideas, which perhaps contributes to it's obvious romance. The Afghan people are still to this day largely a tribal, nomadic race which makes documentation of their activities, dog breeding included, very difficult.

It was towards the end of the 19th century that the Afghan Hound had his beginnings in Britain. Two types of dog were imported from Afghanistan, one being of Saluki type, rangy, with a short silky coat, and a stockier dog with a thick woolly coat. The former was the dog of the plains and the latter was of the mountain regions. Today's Afghan is perhaps closer to the mountain variety although these early specimens bore little resemblance to the present ones.

He is a dog of great speed and agility and, although, not quite as quick as the likes of the Greyhound, there are still some Afghan Hound races to be found.

Their aloof, arrogant air can make these dogs quite difficult to train, much strong willed application being required. The coat, of course, requires an immense amount of attention.

KEY TO CHARACTER	
INTELLIGENCE	***
TEMPERAMENT	***
EASE OF COAT CARE	*
SUITABILITY FOR SMALL DWELLING	*
***** (5) = VERY GOOD	

BRITISH KENNEL CLUB STANDARD

AFGHAN HOUND

CHARACTERISTICS. — The Afghan Hound should be dignified and aloof with a certain keen fierceness. The Eastern or Oriental expression is typical of the breed. The Afghan looks at and through one.

GENERAL APPEARANCE. — The gait of the Afghan Hound should be smooth and springy with a style of high order. The whole appearance of the dog should give the impression of strength and dignity combining speed and power. The head must be held proudly.

Head and Skull. — Skull long, not too narrow with prominent occiput. Foreface long with punishing jaws and slight stop. The skull well balanced and surmounted by a long "top-knot". Nose preferably black but liver is no fault in light coloured dogs.

Eyes. — Should be dark for preference but golden colour is not debarred. Nearly triangular, slanting slightly upwards from the inner corner to the outer.

Ears. — Set low and well back, carried close to the head. Covered with long silky hair.

Mouth. — Level.

Neck. — Long, strong with proud carriage of the head.

Forequarters. — Shoulders long and sloping, well set back, well muscled and strong without being loaded. Forelegs straight and well boned, straight with shoulder, elbows held in.

Body. — Back level, moderate length, well muscled, the back falling slightly away to the stern. Loin straight, broad and rather short. Hip-bones rather prominent and wide apart. A fair spring of ribs and good depth of chest.

Hindquarters. — Powerful, well bent and well turned stifles. Great length between hip and hock with a comparatively short distance between hock and foot. The dew claws may be removed or remain at the discretion of the breeder.

Feet. — Forefeet strong and very large both in length and breadth and covered with long thick hair, toes arched. Pasterns long and springy, especially in front and pads well down on the ground. Hindfeet long, but not quite so broad as forefeet, covered with long thick hair.

Tail. — Not too short. Set on low with ring at the end. Raised when in action. Sparsely feathered.

Coat.— Long and very fine texture on ribs, fore and hind-quarters and flanks. From the shoulder backwards and along the saddle the hair should be short and close in mature dogs. Hair long from the forehead backward, with a distinct silky "top-knot". On the foreface the hair is short as on the back. Ears and legs well coated. Pasterns can be bare. Coat must be allowed to develop naturally.

Colour. — All colours are acceptable.

Weight and Size. — Ideal height: Dogs 68-74cm (27"-29"). Bitches 5-8cm (2"-3") smaller.

Faults. — Any appearance of courseness. Skull too wide and foreface too short. Weak underjaw. Large round or full eyes. Neck should never be too short or thick. Back too long or too short.

Note. — Male animals should have two apparently normal testicles fully descended into the scrotum.

MAIN AMERICAN KENNEL CLUB VARIATION TO STANDARD FOR THE AFGHAN HOUND —

Height. — Dogs, 27 inches, plus or minus one inch; bitches, 25 inches, plus or minus one inch.

Weight. — Dogs, about 60 pounds; bitches about 50 pounds.

AFGHAN HOUND REGISTRATIONS 1981 — 87 INCLUSIVE

1981 — 1187
1982 — 933
1983 — 763
1984 — 911
1985 — 643
1986 — 665
1987 — 645

CRUFTS BEST-IN-SHOW WINNER — 1983 — CH. MONTRAVIA KASKARAK HITARI MRS. P. GIBBS.

BASENJI

This interesting breed was depicted in a similar form in Egyptian tomb paintings dating back to 3600 B.C. Little was known of the progress of these dogs until explorers rediscovered specimens in the Congo and Sudan around 1860. The Africans who kept them valued their hunting ability very highly, using them in packs to flush game into strategically placed nets. Although of only moderate size, the Basenji had the necessary courage and tenacity for this work and some believe he has passed on these traits as a progenitor of modern terriers.

The Basenji is famous as the dog who never barks, instead he emits his own unique sound which is accurately described in the breed standard as a type of yodel. This fascinating characteristic and the extreme cleanliness of the Basenji have helped contribute to a fair size following for the breed in Britain. He is known to be an excellent dog for showing, having a sensible temperament and attractive sleek coat.

In the home he behaves well and his comparitive silence and lack of odour will appeal to many people. He mixes well with children and despite his apparently semi-wild past, he is in fact a thoroughly domesticated dog.

With the Basenji's active history, exercise must be liberal and this will prove to be enjoyable for dog and owner alike, as the Basenji makes a lively companion.

KEY TO CHARACTER	
INTELLIGENCE	***
TEMPERAMENT	****
EASE OF COAT CARE	*****
SUITABILITY FOR SMALL DWELLING	****
***** (5) = VERY GOOD	

BRITISH KENNEL CLUB STANDARD

BASENJI

CHARACTERISTICS. — The Basenji does not bark but is not mute, its own special noise is a mixture of a chortle and a yodel. It is remarkable for its cleanliness in every way. The wrinkled forehead, tightly curled tail, and legs carried straight foreward with a swift, long, tireless, swinging stride, are typical of the breed.

GENERAL APPEARANCE. — The Basenji should be a lightly built, finely boned aristocratic looking animal, high on the leg compared with its length, always poised, alert and intelligent. The wrinkled head, with pricked ears, should be proudly carried on a well-arched neck. The deep brisket should run up into a definite waist and the tail be tightly curled, presenting a picture of a well-balanced dog of gazelle-like grace.

Head and Skull. — The skull should be flat, well-chiselled and of medium width, tapering towards the nose, with only a slight stop. The distance from the top of the head to the stop is slightly more than from the stop to the tip of the nose. The side lines of the skull taper gradually towards the mouth, giving a clean-cheeked appearance. Fine and profuse wrinkles should appear on the forehead when the ears are pricked, side wrinkles are desirable but should not be exaggerated into dewlap. Wrinkles are more noticeable in puppies, but, because of lack of shadowing, are not as noticeable in tri-colours. A black nose is greatly desired.

Eyes. — Dark, almond shaped, obliquely set, far-seeing and rather inscrutable in expression.

Ears. — Small, pointed, erect and slightly hooded, of fine texture, set well forward on top of the head, the tip of the ear should be nearer the centre of the skull than the outside base.

Mouth. — The mouth should be level, with scissors bite, the upper teeth slightly over-lapping and touching the lower teeth.

Neck. — Strong and of good length, without thickness, well-crested and slightly full at the base of the throat with a graceful curve accentuating the crest. It should be well-set into laid back shoulders so as to give the head a "lofty" carriage.

Forequarters. — The shoulders must be well laid back, muscular but not loaded. The points of the scapulae should be fairly close at the withers. The elbows should be firmly tucked in against the brisket. When viewed form in front the elbows should be in line with the ribs and the legs should continue in a straight line to the ground giving a narrow front. The forelegs should be straight with fine bone and very long fore-arms. Pasterns should be of good length, straight but flexible.

Body. — Balanced with short, level back. Ribs well sprung, deep and oval. The join short-coupled and the deep brisket running up into a definite waist.

Hindquarters. — Strong and muscular, with hocks well let down, turned neither in nor out, with long second thighs and moderately bent stifles.

Feet. — Small, narrow and compact, with deep pads, well-arched toes and short nails.

Tail. — The tail should be high set with the posterior curve of the buttock extending beyond the root of the tail giving a reachy appearance to the hindquarters. The tail curls tightly over the spine and lies closely to the thigh with a single or double curl.

Coat. — Short, sleek and close, very fine. Skin very pliant.

Colour. — Pure bright red, or pure black, or black and tan, all with white feet, chest and tail tips. White legs, white blaze and white collar optional.

Size and Weight. — Ideal heights. Dogs 43cm (17″) at shoulder; Bitches 40cm (16″); a few cm (an inch) either way should not penalize an otherwise well-balanced specimen. Ideal weights: Dogs 11Kg (24lbs), Bitches 9½Kg (21lbs).

Faults. — Coarse, domed or peaked skull. Muzzle too long or too broad. Cheekiness. Mouth over-shot or under-shot. Round or light eyes. Ears too low-set or too large. Wide chest, barrel ribs, shelly brisket. Short in the leg, out at elbows, toeing in. Heavy bone, cow hocks, low-set or straight tail, thin flat open feet. Long or heavy coat. Creams, sables, or any other colours than those defined in the Colour paragraph above should be heavily penalised. Poor temperament.

Note. — Male animals should have two apparently normal testicles fully descended into the scrotum.

BASENJI REGISTRATIONS 1981 — 87 INCLUSIVE

1981 —	67
1981 —	83
1983 —	132
1984 —	91
1985 —	66
1986 —	93
1987 —	121

YET TO WIN CRUFTS BEST-IN-SHOW.

BASSET HOUND

The Basset Hound is one of the most instantly recognisable breeds in Britain. It's unique form and various advertising appearances have ensured a growing popularity in recent years.

He is a direct descendant of the St. Hubert Hound of France. This truly ancient breed was developed in the Ardennes region by the man who lent his name to it, Hubert, who was an abbot. Although a man of the cloth, he had a great passion for hunting, and wanted a hound who was capable of following a scent in the dense undergrowth of the area. This was a difficult task for long-legged hounds who had to stoop continuously. So the short-legged Basset type dog was developed the words "Bas set" meaning low set in French. These hounds eventually spread throughout France and various forms of the breed began to appear, but all were of the shorter-legged variety. Several of these dogs were imported by the English, and after careful cross-breeding, the Basset Hound was registered in 1883.

Although he is the slowest of the hounds, in the field he is one of the most thorough and consistent workers. He is fundamentally a gentle, easy going character, rarely attacking game when he has located it.

In the home he fits well into any family environment, being faithful and affectionate. Despite his apparently sluggish disposition, he does require a fair amount of exercise to avoid laziness and obesity.

Bassett Hound
Beagle

Bloodhound
Borzoi

KEY TO CHARACTER	
INTELLIGENCE	***
TEMPERAMENT	*****
EASE OF COAT CARE	*****
SUITABILITY FOR SMALL DWELLING	**
***** (5) = VERY GOOD	

BRITISH KENNEL CLUB STANDARD

BASSET HOUND

GENERAL CHARACTERISTICS. — A short-legged hound of considerable substance, well-balanced and full of quality. Action is most important. A smooth free action with forelegs reaching well forward and hind legs showing powerful thrust and the hound moving true both front and rear. Hocks and stifles must not be stiff in movement nor must any toes be dragged.

Head and Skull. — Domes, with some stop and the occipital bone prominent; of medium width at the brow and tapering slightly to the muzzle; the general appearance of the foreface is lean but not snipy. The top of the muzzle nearly parallel with the line from stop to occiput and not much longer than the head from stop to occiput. There may be a moderate amount of wrinkle at the brows and beside the eyes and in any event the skin of the head should be so loose as to wrinkle noticeably when drawn forward or when the head is lowered. The flews of the upper lip overlap the lower substantially.

Nose. — Entirely black, except in light-coloured hounds, when it may be brown or liver. Large with well opened nostrils and may protrude a little beyond the lips.

Eyes. — Brown, but may shade to hazel in light-coloured hounds, neither prominent nor too deep set. The expression is calm and serious and the red of the lower lid appears, though not exceedingly.

Ears. — Set on low but not excessively so and never above the line of the eye, very long, reaching at least to the end of a muzzle of correct length, narrow throughout their length and curling well inwards; very supple, fine and velvety in texture.

Mouth. — The teeth level with a scissors bite although if they meet edge to edge it is not a fault.

Neck. — Muscular and fairly long with pronounced dewlap but not exaggerated.

Forequarters. — Shoulder-blades well laid back and shoulders not heavy. Forelegs short, powerful and with great bone, the elbows turned neither out nor in but fitting easily against the side. The knees at least slightly crooked inwards but not to so great an extent as to prevent free action or to result in legs touching each other when standing or in action. Knuckling-over is a bad fault. There may be wrinkles of skin between knee and foot.

Body. — The breast bone slightly prominent but the chest not narow or unduly deep; the ribs well-rounded and sprung and carried well back. The back rather broad, level, and with withers and quarters of approximately the same height, though the loins may arch slightly. The back from withers to the inset of the quarters not unduly long.

Hindquarters. — Full of muscle and standing out well, giving an almost spherical effect when viewing the hound from the rear. Stifles well bent. The hocks as low to the ground as possible and lightly bent under the hound but not turned in or out. They should be placed just under the body when standing naturally. One or two wrinkles of skin may appear between hock and foot and at the rear of the joint a slight pouch resulting from the looseness of the skin.

Feet. — Massive well knuckled-up and padded. Thre forefeet may point straight ahead or be turned slighly outwards but in every case the hound must stand perfectly true, the weight being borne equally by toes with pads together so that the feet would leave the imprint of a large hound and no unpadded areas in contact with the ground.

Tail. — Well set-on, rather long, strong at the base and tapering with a moderate amount of coarse hair underneath. When the hound is moving the stern is carried well up and curves gently sabre-fashion over the back but is never curling or gay.

Coat. — Smooth short and close without being too fine. The whole outline should be clean and free from feathering. The presence of a long-haired soft coat, with feathering, is very undesirable.

Colour. — Generally black, white and tan or lemon and white, but any recognised hound colour is acceptable.

Height. — Height 33-38cm (13"-15").

Faults. — Any departure from the foregoing points should be considered a fault and the seriousness with which the fault should be regarded should be in exact proportion to its degree.

Note. — Male animals should have two apparently normal testicles full descended into the scrotum.

MAIN AMERICAN KENNEL CLUB VARIATION TO STANDARD FOR THE BASSET HOUND —

Size. — The height should not exceed 14 inches. Height over 15 inches at the highest point of the shoulder blades is a disqualification.

BASSET HOUND REGISTRATONS 1981 — 87 INCLUSIVE

1981 — 713
1982 — 659
1983 — 626
1984 — 609
1985 — 737
1986 — 641
1987 — 657

YET TO WIN CRUFTS BEST-IN-SHOW.

Long-Haired Dachshund

BEAGLE

First mention of the Beagle was in the fifteenth century and it is widely believed that he goes back a great deal further than that, some saying that a similar dog existed in the third century.

He is a hound of beautiful proportions, having the Basset's advantage of being close to the ground, whilst being very speedy over any terrain. He is chunky and tireless, showing great exuberance when hunting. They are one of the most esteemed scent hounds among huntsmen as they have very few faults in their makeup.

There used to be a liking amongst some breeders for packs of miniature Beagles, even royalty have bred such packs. But these dwarf dogs have become increasingly rare, and in fact the last century has seen an overall increase in the size of the breed.

The hound used for the hunt tends to differ from the show dog, the latter being more compact with a larger skull.

The Beagle makes a marvellous family dog, with no malice or untrustworthiness. His often striking markings and expressive face make him very popular with children and adults alike. Exercise should be frequent and he will especially appreciate running with other dogs.

KEY TO CHARACTER	
INTELLIGENCE	***
TEMPERAMENT	*****
EASE OF COAT CARE	*****
SUITABILITY FOR SMALL DWELLING	***
***** (5) = VERY GOOD	

BRITISH KENNEL CLUB STANDARD

BEAGLE

CHARACTERISTICS. — A merry hound whose essential function is to hunt, primarily hare, by following a scent. Bold with great activity, stamina and detrmination. Alert, intelligent and of even temperament.

GENERAL APPEARANCE. — A sturdy and compactly-built hound, conveying the impression of quality without coarseness.

Head and Skull. — Head fair length, powerful in the dog without being coarse, but finer in the bitch; free from frown and excessive wrinkle. Skull slightly domed, moderately wide, with indication of peak. Stop well defined and dividing length between occiput and top of nose as equally as possible. Muzzle not snipy, lips reasonably well flewed. Nose broad and nostrils well expanded; preferably black, but less pigmentation permissible in the lighter coloured hounds.

Eyes. — Dark brown or hazel, fairly large, not deep set or bulgy, set well apart and with a mild appealing expression.

Ears. — Long with round tip, reaching nearly to end of nose when drawn out. Set on low, fine in texture and hanging gracefully close to cheek.

Mouth. — *Teeth strongly developed. Upper incisors just overlapping and touching outer surface of lower incisors to form scissor bite.*

Neck. — Sufficiently long to enable hound to come down easily to scent, slightly arched and showing a little dewlap.

Forequarters. — Shoulder clean and sloping. Forelegs straight and upright, well under the hound, of good substance, strong, hard and round in bone. Not tapering off to feet. Pasterns short. Elbows firm, turning neither in nor out. Height to elbow about half the hound's height to withers.

Body. — Topline straight and level. Chest well let down to below elbow. Ribs well sprung and extending well back. Short between the couplings. Loins powerful and supple, without excessive tuck-up.

Hindquarters. — Very muscular about the thighs. Stifles well bent. Hocks firm, well let down and parallel to each other.

Feet. — Tight and firm. Well knuckled up and strongly padded. Not hare-footed. Nails short.

Gait. — Back level and no roll. Stride free, long-reaching and straight without high action. Hind legs showing drive. Should not move close behind or paddle or plait in front.

Tail. — Sturdy and moderate length. Set on high and carried gaily but not curled over back or inclined forward from the root. Well covered with hair, especially on underside.

Coat. — Short, dense and weatherproof.

Colour. — Any recognised hound colour other than liver. Tip of stern white.

Weight and Size. — It is desirable that height from ground to withers should neither exceed 40cm (16″) nor fall below 33cm (13″).

Note. — Male animals should have two apparently normal testicles fully descended into the scrotum.

MAIN AMERICAN KENNEL CLUB VARIATION TO STANDARD FOR THE BEAGLE —

Two size varieties. — Thirteen Inch — which shall be for hounds not exceeding 13 inches in height. Fifteen inch — which shall be for hounds over 13 but not exceeding 15 inches in height.

BEAGLE REGISTRATONS 1981 — 1987 INCLUSIVE

1981 — 1134
1982 — 943
1983 — 915
1984 — 947
1985 — 1012
1986 — 940
1987 — 780

YET TO WIN CRUFTS BEST-IN-SHOW.

BLOODHOUND

This is one of the very ancient breeds and he can be linked directly to a dog of some 1300 years ago. This was the St. Hubert hound of France, an excellent scent hound which was later introduced to England by William the Conqueror. This breed was then developed into the Talbot Hound. It is the Talbot Hound which lends it's name to so many inns throughout Britain and early descriptions of the breed suggest a fair resemblance to the modern Bloodhound.

The Bloodhound was one of the 40 breeds that were entered in the first Kennel Club stud book of 1874 and although he has become an instantly recognisable and well-liked breed, he is not kept in great numbers as a pet.

His great forte, of course, is his amazing scenting power in open countryside. No other dog can follow an old, weak scent as efficiently as the Bloodhound and in particularly difficult cases of criminal detection, the police often turn to his expertise.

Despite his rather gruesome sounding name, the Bloodhound is one of the gentlest dogs imaginable. Children are totally safe in his company, as he is patient and affectionate. Anyone with sufficient space and the inclination for long exercise spells in the country will find him a model companion.

KEY TO CHARACTER	
INTELLIGENCE	*****
TEMPERAMENT	*****
EASE OF COAT CARE	*****
SUITABILITY FOR SMALL DWELLING	*
***** (5) = VERY GOOD	

BRITISH KENNEL CLUB STANDARD

BLOODHOUND

CHARACTERISTICS. — The Bloodhound possesses in a most marked degree every point and characteristic of those dogs which hunt together by scent (Sagaces). He is very powerful and stands over more ground than is usual with hounds of other breeds. The skin is thin and extremely loose, this being especially noticeable about the head and neck, where it hangs in deep folds. In temperament he is affectionate, neither quarrelsome with companions nor with other dogs. His nature is somewhat reserved and sensitive.

GENERAL APPEARANCE. — The expression is noble and dignified and characterized by solemnity, wisdom and power. The gait is elastic, swinging and free; the stern being carried high scimitar fashion.

Head and Skull. — The head is narrow in proportion to its length and long in proportion to the body, tapering but slightly from the temples to the muzzle, thus (when viewed from above and in front) having the appearance of being flattened at the sides and of being nearly equal in width throughout its entire length. In profile the upper outline of the skull is nearly in the same plane as that of the foreface. The length from the end of the nose to stop (midway between the eyes) should not be less than that from stop to back or occipital protuberance (peak). The entire length of head from the posterior part of the occipital protuberance to the end of the muzzle should be 30cm (12″) or more in dogs and 28cm (11″) or more in bitches. The skull is long and narrow, with the occipital peak very pronounced. The brows are not prominent although owing to the deep-set eyes they may have that appearance. The foreface is long, deep and of even width throughout, with square outlines when seen in profile. The head is furnished with an amount of loose skin, which in nearly every position appears superabundant, but more particularly so when the head is carried low; the skin then falls into loose pendulous ridges and folds, especially over the forehead and sides of the face. The nostrils are large and open. In front the lips fall squarely making a right angle with the upper line of the foreface; whilst behind they form deep hanging flews, and, being continued into the pendant folds of loose skin about the neck, constitute the dewlap, which is very pronounced.

Mouth. — A scissor bite with the inner faces of the upper incisors touching the outer faces of the lower incisors.

Eyes. — The eyes are deeply sunk in the orbits, the lids assuming a lozenge or diamond shape, in consequence of the lower lids being dragged down and everted by the heavy flews. The eyes correspond with the general colour of the animal varying from deep hazel to yellow. The hazel colour is however to be preferred, although very seldom seen in liver and tan (red and tan) hounds. The eye should be free from any interference from the eyelashes.

Ears. — The ears are thin and soft to the touch, extremely long, set on very low and fall in graceful folds, the lower parts curling inwards and backwards.

Neck. — Should be long.

Forequarters. — The shoulders muscular and well sloped backwards. The forelegs are straight, large and round in bone with elbows squarely set. The pasterns should be strong.

Hindquarters. — The thighs and second thighs (gaskins) are very muscular, the hocks well bent and let down and squarely set.

Feet. — Should be strong and well knuckled up.

Body. — The ribs are well sprung and the chest well let down between the forelegs forming a deep keel. The back and loins are strong, the latter deep and slightly arched.

Tail. — The stern is long and thick tapering to a point, set on high with a moderate amount of hair underneath. It should be carried scimitar fashion, but not curled over the back or corkscrew at any time.

Colour. — The colours are balck and tan, liver and tan (red and tan) and red. The darker colours being sometimes interspersed with lighter or badger-coloured hair and sometimes flecked with white. A small amount of white is permissible on chest, feet and tip of stern.

Weight and Size. — The mean average height of adult dogs is 66cm (26″) and of bitches 61cm (24″). Dogs usually vary from 63-69cm (25″-27″) and bitches from 58-63cm (23″-25″). The mean average weight of adult dogs in fair condition is 41Kg (90lbs) and of adult bitches 36Kg (80lbs). Dogs attain the weight of 50Kg (110lbs) and bitches 45Kg (100lbs). Hounds of the maximum height and weight are to be preferred providing always that quality, proportion and balance combine.

Note. — Male animals should have two apparently normal testicles fully descended into the scrotum.

BLOODHOUND REGISTRATONS 1981 — 1987 INCLUSIVE

1981 —   90
1982 — 113
1983 —   90
1984 —   83
1985 — 140
1986 —   91
1987 — 114

YET TO WIN CRUFTS BEST-IN-SHOW.

BORZOI

The Borzoi has all the classic features of the Greyhound group, taut muscular limbs, long narrow skull and a high arched back, the trademark of the speediest dogs.

The breed is of Russian origin and very ancient. Although there are other theories, it seems very possible that today's Borzoi came from the crossing of one of several coursing hounds used in Russia in the 17th and 18th centuries, with a massive breed called a Liptok. The longer coated of the dogs resulting from this cross were called Psovi Borzois, which is the type we are now familiar with.

Borzois were rarely taken as pets by the Russian people of the time as they were mainly employed, very effectively, as wolf coursing dogs. This was an enormously popular pursuit with well heeled noblemen and was performed with great ceremony and spectacle. The Revolution of 1917 naturally saw the last of these hunts and the Borzoi entered a serious decline, so serious in fact, that extinction threatened. But dedicated enthusiasts rallied to the problem and gradually bolstered the numbers.

The first Borzois seen in England came in the latter half of the 19th century and were then called Russian Wolfhounds, the Borzoi club proper being formed in 1892

It would be wrong to suggest to a prospective owner that the Borzoi is the easiest dog to train but with perseverance he can become a rewarding member of the household. People with little space or time for exercise, however, should never consider this breed.

KEY TO CHARACTER	
INTELLIGENCE	***
TEMPERAMENT	**
EASE OF COAT CARE	**
SUITABILITY FOR SMALL DWELLING	*
***** (5) = VERY GOOD	

BRITISH KENNEL CLUB STANDARD

BORZOI

GENERAL APPEARANCE. — A very graceful, aristocratic and elegant dog possessing courage, muscular power and great speed.

Head and Skull. — Head, long and lean. Well filled in below the eyes. Measurement equal from the occiput to the inner corner of the eye and from the inner corner of the eye to tip of nose. Skull very slightly domed and narrow, stop not perceptible, inclining to Roman nose. Head fine so that the direction of the bones and principal veins can be clearly seen. Bitches heads should be finer than the dogs. Jaws long, deep and powerful; nose large and black, not pink or brown, nicely rounded, neither cornered nor sharp. Viewed from above the skull should look narrow, converging very gradually to top of nose.

Eyes. — Dark, intelligent, alert and keen. Almond shaped, set obliquely, placed well back but not too far apart, Eye rims dark, Eyes should not be light, round or staring.

Ears. — Small and fine in quality; not too far apart. They should be active and responsive; when alert can be erect; when in repose nearly touching at the occiput.

Mouth. — The jaws should be strong, with a perfect, regular and complete scissor bite, i.e. the upper teeth closely overlappi ng the lower teeth and set square to the jaws.

Neck. — Clean, slightly arched; reasonably long. Well set on, free from throatiness. Flat at the sides, not round.

Forequarters. — Shoulders clean, sloping well back, fine at withers, free from lumpiness. Forelegs, lean and straight. Seen from the front, narrow like blades; from the side, wide at shoulder narrowing down to foot; elbows neither turned in nor out, pasterns strong, flexible and springy.

Body. — Chest, great depth of brisket, rather narrow. Ribs well sprung and flexible; neither flat sided nor barrel-shaped; very deep giving heart room and lung play, especially in the case of mature males. (It is from depth of chest rather than breadth that the Borzoi derives its heart room and lung play). Back, rising in a graceful arch from as near the shoulder as possible with a well balanced fall-away. The arch to be more marked in dogs than bitches. Rather bony, muscular and free from any cavity. Muscles, highly developed and well distributed.

Hindquarters. — Loins, broad and very powerful, with plenty of muscular development. Quarters should be wider than shoulders, ensuring stability of stance. Thighs long, well developed with good second thigh. Hind-legs, long, muscular, stifles well bent, hocks broad, clean and well let down.

Feet. — Front feet rather long, toes close together; well arched, never flat, neither turning in nor out. Hind feet hare-like, i.e., longer and less arched.

Tail. — Long, rather low set. Well feathered, carried low, not gaily. In action may be used as rudder but not rising above level of back. From the level of the hocks may be sickle shaped but not ringed.

Coat. — Long and silky (never woolly), or flat, or wavy, or rather curly. Short and smooth on head, ears and front legs; on the neck the frill profuse and rather curly; forelegs and chest well feathered; on hind-quarters and tail, long and profuse feathering.

Weight and Size. — Height at shoulder; Dogs from 74cm (29") upwards. Bitches from 68cm (27") upwards.

Note. — Male animals should have two apparently normal testicles fully descended into the scrotum.

MAIN AMERICAN KENNEL CLUB VARIATION TO THE STANDARD FOR BORZOI —

Size. — Mature males should be at least 28 inches at the withers and mature bitches at least 26 inches at the withers. Range in weight for males from 75 to 105 pounds and for bitches from 15 to 20 pounds less.

BORZOI REGISTRATIONS 1981 — 87 INCLUSIVE

1981 — 206
1982 — 158
1983 — 269
1984 — 246
1985 — 180
1986 — 240
1987 — 244

YET TO WIN CRUFTS BEST-IN-SHOW.

DACHSHUND

The first specimens of this breed to appear were almost certainly the Smooth-haired type. Developed in Germany where it was first called the 'Teckel', the Dachshund was first and foremost a burrowing dog used for the hunting of badgers and foxes. It is thought that similar dogs have been used in this way for over four centuries and it is not difficult to see why. The shape of the Dachshund is unique, having very short strong legs and a long muscular body, with which he can writhe and dig with great effectiveness in a confined space.

The German people well and truly took the Dachshund to their hearts, to the point in fact where he became their national dog. This, unfortunately, worked against the breed when, during and just after World War I, anything remotely Teutonic in origin was despised by the rest of Europe, so the poor Dachshund was reviled for some time. But that ridiculous situation is mere history now, and he is a much loved breed all over the world.

There are two other types of coat in the Dachshund family, the Long-haired and the Wire-haired. The former is thought to have resulted from the introduction of Spaniel blood and possibly some outcrossing with an ancient German breed called the Stöberhund. The Wire-haired variety comes from the crossing of Smooth-haired Dachshunds with Dandie Dinmont and Scottish Terriers.

In the home he is normally well-behaved, affectionate and loyal. Small children, though should be discouraged from teasing him as he can have a fairly aggressive streak. He barks with great vigour and makes a forceful guard despite his size. Great care should be taken not to overfeed, as overweight Dachshunds are often known to suffer with spinal problems. A moderate amount of daily exercise should always be given.

KEY TO CHARACTER	
INTELLIGENCE	***
TEMPERAMENT	****
EASE OF COAT CARE	
Smooth-haired	*****
Long-haired	***
Wire-haired	****
SUITABILITY FOR	*****
SMALL DWELLING	

***** (5) = VERY GOOD

BRITISH KENNEL CLUB STANDARD

DACHSHUND (Long-Haired)

CHARACTERISTICS. — The long-haired Dachshund is an old, fixed sub-variety of the "Teckel", and its history extends back to the beginning of Teckel breeding. The breed is full of character, quick in attack and defence, faithful when properly brough up and very obedient. All the senses are well developed. It has the reputation of being extraordinarily intelligent and easy to train. Its build and temperament fit it to hunt quarry both above and below ground; its eagerness, keen sight and hearing and its sonorous bark make it especially suitable for tracking. In these respects it compares very favourably with any other variety. The thick, soft hair protects it against thorns, enables it to endure both cold and heat and is rain-proof. It is especially suited to water work. In following a trail to retrieve. The long-haired Dachshund can therefore be used in many different ways by the sportsman.

GENERAL APPEARANCE. — Form, colour, size and character similar in all respects to those of the smooth Dachshund, except for the long, soft hair. The form is compact, short-legged and long, but sinewy and well muscled, with bold and defiant head carriage, and intelligent expression. In spite of the shortness of the legs the body should be neither too plump nor so slender as to have weasel-like appearance. Height at shoulder should be half the length of the body measured from breast bone to the set-on of the tail, and the girth of the chest double the height at the shoulder. The length from the tip of the nose to the eyes should be equal to the length from the eyes to the base of the skull. The tail should not touch the ground when at rest, neither should the ears (i.e., the leather) extend beyond the nose when pulled to the front.

Head and Skull. — Long and conical when seen from above, and in profile, sharp and finely modelled. Skull neither too broad nor too narrow, only slightly arched, without prominent stop. Foreface long and narrow, finely modelled. Lips should be tightly drawn, well covering the lower jaw, neither too heavy nor too sharply cut away, the corners of the mouth slightly marked.

Eyes. — Medium in size, oval, set obliquely, clear, expressive and dark in colour.

Ears. — Broad and placed, relatively well back, high and well set on lying close to the cheeks, broad and long, nicley feathered and very mobile.

Mouth. — Wide, extending back to behind the eyes, furnished with strong teeth which should fit into one another exactly, the inner side of the upper incisors closing on the outer side of the under ones.

Neck. — Sufficiently long, muscular, showing no dewlap, slightly arched at the nape, running gracefully into the shoulders, carried well up and forward.

Forequarters. — Muscular, with deep chest. Shoulders long and broad, set obliquely, lying firmly on well developed ribs. Muscles hard and plastic. Breast bone prominent, extending so far forward as to show depressions on both sides. Upper arm the same length as the shoulder blade, jointed at right angles to the shoulder, well boned and muscled, set on close to the ribs but moving freely as far as the shoulder blade. Lower arm comparatively short, inclined slightly inwards, solid and well muscled.

Body. — Long and well muscled, the back showing oblique shoulders and short and strong pelvic region. Ribs very oval, deep between the fore-legs and extending far back. Loin short, strong and broad. The line of the back only slightly depressed over the shoulders and slightly arched over the loin, with the ouline of the belly moderately tucked up.

Hindquarters. — Rump round, full broad, with muscles well modelled and plastic. Pelvis bone not too short, broad, strongly developed and set obliquely. Thigh bone strong, of good length and jointed to the pelvis at right angles. Second thigh short, set at right angles to the upper thigh, well muscled. Hocks set wide apart, strongly bent and, seen from behind, the legs should be straight.

Feet. — Broad and large, straight or turned slightly outwards; the hind feet smaller and narrower than the fore. Toes close together and with a distinct arch to each toe. Nails strong. The dog must stand equally on all parts of the foot.

Tail. — Set on fairly high, not too long, tapering and without too marked a curve. Not carried too high. Fully feathered.

Coat. — Soft and straight or slightly waved, of shining colour. Longer under the neck, the underparts of the body and, particularly, on the ears, behind the legs, where it should develop into abundant feathering, and reach the greatest length on the tail, where it should form a flag. The feathering should extend to the outsides of the ears, where short hair is not desired. Too heavy a coat gives an appearance of undue plumpness and hides the outline. The coat should resemble that of an Irish Setter, giving the dog an appearance of elegance. Too much hair on the feet is ugly and useless.

Colour. — Black and tan, dark brown with lighter shadings, dark red, light red, dappled, tiger-marked or brindle. In Black and tan, red and dappled dogs the nose and nails should be black, in chocolate they are often brown.

Weight and Size. — As a rule Long-Haired Dachshunds are classified as follows:- Middle weight up to 7.7Kg (17 lbs) for bitches and 8.2Kg (18 lbs) for dogs. Heavy weight over 7.7Kg (17 lbs) for bitches and over 8.2Kg (18 lbs) for dogs. The Middle-weights are best suited for badger and fox drawing and the Heavy-weights for tracking, hunting larger animals and for water work. The last named are also very useful for retrieving rabbits and water fowl.

Note. — Male animals should have two apparently normal testicles fully descended into the scrotum.

DACHSHUND (Smooth-Haired)

CHARACTERISTICS. — First and foremost a sporting dog, the Smooth Dachshund is remarkably versatile, being equally adaptable as a house pet; his smooth, close coat is impervious to rain and mud. His temperament and acute intelligence make him the ideal companion for town or country. In the field of sport he is unequalled, combining the scenting powers of a Foxhound with unflinching courage, and will go to ground to fox, otter or badger.

GENERAL APPEARANCE. — Long and low, but with compact and well-muscled body, not crippled, cloddy, or clumsy, with bold defiant carriage of head and intelligent expression.

Head and Skull. — Long and appearing conical when seen from above, and, from a side view tapering to the point of the muzzle. Stop not pronounced, skull should be slightly arched in profile, appearing neither too broad nor too narrow. Jaw neigher too square nor snipy but strong, the lips lightly stretched fairly covering the lower jaw.

Eyes. — Medium in size, oval, and set obliquely. Dark in colour, except in the case of Chocolates, in which they may be lighter; in Dapples one or both wall eyes are permissible.

Ears. — Broad, of moderate length, and well rounded (not narrow, pointed or folded), relatively well back, high and well set on, lying close to the cheek, very mobile as in all intelligent dogs; when at attention the back of the ear directed forward and outward.

Mouth. — Teeth must be strongly developed. The powerful canine teeth must fit closely. The correct bite is a scissors bite, any deviation being a fault.

Neck. — Sufficiently long, muscular, clean, no dewlap, slightly arched in the nape, running in graceful lines into the shoulders, carried well up and forward.

Forequarters. — Shoulder blades long, broad and set on sloping, lying firmly on fully-developed ribs, muscles hard and plastic. Chest very oval, with ample room for the heart and lungs, deep and with ribs well sprung out towards the loins, breast-bone very prominent. The front legs should, when viewed from one side, cover the lowest point of the breastline. Forelegs very short andin proportion to size strong in bone. Upper arm of equal length with, and at right angles to, the shoulder blade; elbows lying close to ribs, but moving freely up to shoulder blades. Lower arm short as compared with other animals, slightly inclined inwards (crook), seen in profile moderately straight; not bending forward or knuckling over (which indicates unsoundness).

Body. — Long and muscular, the line of back slighly depressed at shoulders and slightly arched over the loin, which should be short and strong; outline of belly moderately tucked up. What is required is a general levelness of the back, the hindquarters (the rump) not being higher than the shoulders.

Hindquarters. — Rump round, full, broad; muscles hard and plastic; hip bone or pelvic bone not too short, broad and strongly developed, set moderately sloping, thigh bones strong, of good length, and joined to pelvis at right-angles; lower thighs short in comparison with other animals; hocks well developed and seen from behind the legs should be straight (not cow-hocked). The dog should not appear higher at the quarters than at shoulders.

Feet. — The front feet should be full, broad and close-knit, and straight or very slightly turned outwards, the hind feet smaller and narrower. The toes must be close together with a decided arch to each toe, with strong regularly placed nails and firm pads. The dog must stand true, i.e., equally on all parts of the foot.

Tail. — Set on fairly high, strong and tapering, but not too long and not too curved or carried too high.

Coat. — Short, dense and smooth, but strong. The hair on the underside of the tail course in texture; skin loose and supply, but fitting the dog closely all over, without much wrinkle.

Colour. — Any colour other than white (except a white spot on breast). Nose and nails should be black. In red dogs a red nose is permissible but not desirable. In Chocolate and Dapples the nose may be brown or flesh-coloured. In Dapples large spots of colour are undesirable, and the dog should be evenly dappled all over.

Weight and Size. — Dogs should not exceed 11.3Kg (25 lbs). Bitches should not exceed 10.4Kg (23 lbs).

Faults. — In general appearance weak or deformed, too high or too low to the ground; ears set on too high or too low, eyes too prominent; muzzle too short or pinched, either undershot or overshot; forelegs too crooked; hare or terrier feet, or flat spread toes (flat-footed); out at elbows; body too much dip behind the shoulders; loins weak or too arched; chest too flat or too short; hindquarters weak or cow-hocked, quarters higher than the shoulders.

Note. — Male animals should have two apparently normal testicles fully descended into the scrotum.

DACHSHUND (Wire-Haired)

CHARACTERISTICS. — The Dachshund should be clever, lively, courageous to the point of rashness, sagacious and obedient. He is especially suited for going to ground because of his low build, very strong forequarters and forelegs, long, strong jaw, and the immense power of his bite and hold. His loose skin enables him to manoeuvre with ease for attack or defence. His deep, loud bay indicates his position to those working him. He is also well equipped for field work on account of his good nose and sound construction. He can force his way through cover so dense that it would stop even the smallest gundog. Because of his nose, voice, good sight and perseverence he makes a good tracking dog.

GENERAL APPEARANCE. — Low to ground, short legged, the body long but compact and well muscled. The head should be carried boldly and the expression be very intelligent. Despite his short legs, compared with the length of this body, he must not be awkward, cramped, crippled or lacking in substance.

Head and Skull. — Looked at from above or from the side, the head should taper uniformly to the tip of the nose and be clean cut. The skull is only slightly arched, being neither too broad nor too narrow and slopes gradually, without marked stop, to a finely formed, slightly arched muzzle, the nasal bones and cartilage (Septum) being long and narrow. The ridges of the frontal bones are well developed giving prominence to the nerve bosses over the eyes. Jaw has extremely strong bones, is very long and opens very wide. It should not be too square nor yet snipy. The lips are lightly stretched, the corners just marked and the upper lip covers the lower jaw neatly.

Eyes. — Oval, medium size, set obliquely, lustrous and expressive. The colour should be dark except in the case of Chocolates, when they may be lighter, and of Dapples, when one or both wall eyes are allowed.

Ears. — Broad and rounded, the front edge touching the cheek. They are relatively well back and high and are well set on. The length is such at when the ears are pulled forward they reach a point approximately half-way between the eyes and the tip of the nose.

Mouth. — The powerful canine teeth fit closely. The correct bite is a scissor bite, any deviation being a fault.

Neck. — Sufficiently long, muscular, clean cut, not showing any dewlap, slightly arched in the nape, extending in a graceful line into the shoulders and carried erect.

Forequarters. — The shoulder blades are long, broad and placed firmly and obliquely upon a very robust rib cage. The upper arm is the same length as the shoulder blade, set at right angles to it and, like the shoulder blade, is very strong and covered with hard but supple muscles. The upper arm lies close to the ribs and is able to move freely. The forearm is comparatively short, inclined slightly inwards to form the crook, when seen in profile is moderately straight and must not bend forward or knuckle over, a state which indicates unsoundness. A correctly placed front leg covers the lowest point of the breast bone.

Body. — The breast bone is strong and prominent enough to show a dimple at each side. Looked at from the front the thorax should be very oval allowing ample room for the heart and lungs; seen from the side it should intersect the forearm just above the wrist. The top line, very slightly depressed at the shoulders and slightly arched over the loin, is parallel to the ground. The whole trunk should be long, well ribbed up and underneath should merge gradually into the line of a moderately tucked up belly. The rump is full, round and wide with strong and pliant muscles.

Hindquarters. — The pelvis is strong, set obliquely and not too short. The upper thigh, set at right angles to the pelvis, is strong and of good length, the lower this is short, set at right angles to the upper thigh and is well muscled. The hocks are well developed. The legs when seen from behind, are set well apart, straight and parallel to one another.

Feet. — The front feet are full, broad in front, straight or turned just a trifle outwards. The four toes forming the foot are compact, well arched and have tough pads. The fifth toe (dewclaw) is usually left on. The nails are strong and short. The dog must stand true and equally on all parts of the foot. The hind feet are smaller and narrower than the fore feet and placed straight. There should be no dewclaw. In all other respects the hind feed and toe are similar to the fore feet and toes.

Tail. — Continues line of the spine; is but slightly curved, must not be carried too gaily or reach the ground when at rest.

Coat. — With the exception of the jaw, eyebrows and ears, the whole body is covered with a completely even, short, harsh coat and an undercoat. There should be a beard on the chin. The eyebrows are bushy. The hair on the ears is almost smooth.

Colour. — All colours are allowed but a white patch on the chest, though not a fault, is not desirable. Except in the case of Chocolates, when it may be brown or flesh-coloured, the nose should be black.

Weight and Size. — It is recommended that dogs should weigh from 9 to 10Kg (20 to 22 lbs) and bitches from 8.2Kg — 9Kg (18 to 20 lbs).

Faults. — PRIMARY FAULTS. — An overshot or undershot jaw. Out at elbow. Knuckling over. Toes turned inwards. Splayed feet. Cow hocks. A bad coat. SECONDARY FAULTS. — Very light eyes. A narrow chest. Breast bone insufficiently prominent. A dip behind the shoulders. A hollow back. A roach back. Rump higher than withers. Weak loins. Excessively drawn up flanks. Bad angulation of forequarters or hindquarters. Legs too long, too close in front, or behind. Toes turned too much outwards. Bowed hind legs. A sluggish, clumsy or waddling gait. Poor muscle. Too long a tail. MINOR FAULTS. — Ears too high, too low, sticking out, folded or narrow. Too marked a stop. Head too wide, too narrow or too short. Too pointed or too weak a jaw. Short neck or swan neck. Dewlaps. Goggle eyes. Too short a tail.

Note. — Male animals should have two apparently normal testicles full descended into the scrotum.

DACHSHUND REGISTRATIONS 1981 — 87 INCLUSIVE

	LONG-HAIRED	SMOOTH-HAIRED	WIRE-HAIRED
1981 - -	490	444	284
1982 —	466	362	160
1983 —	509	395	240
1984 —	437	372	249
1985 —	462	303	217
1986 —	375	333	265
1987 —	352	304	224

NO DACHSHUND HAS YET WON CRUFTS BEST-IN-SHOW.

MINIATURE DACHSHUND

The Dachshund was always used primarily for the hunting of badger and fox and his German breeders always kept this thought uppermost in their minds. He was developed into the ideal burrowing dog and there was no reason to alter his basic shape and character. But a certain group of hunting men decided that they would like to introduce a scaled-down version of this successful breed for the pursuit of smaller game, mainly rabbits. There were some attempts to outcross with other breeds to produce the desired size but this did not prove as satisfactory as selective breeding from small Dachshund specimens.

Modern Miniature Dachshunds are virtually exact replicas of their larger relatives and so share all their commendable points. All three coat types of this breed make fine show dogs as they all display great confidence and charisma and if presented well can often hold their own against larger hounds.

The obvious advantages that go with such a small dog make him an excellent companion for an elderly or infirm owner or for anyone with limited space. Although he is not a breed who takes easily to strangers, he is normally a good-natured and playful dog. He is very loyal and protective and can produce a surprisingly loud bark when required to guard.

Although the Miniature Dachshund does not require a huge amount of exercise, a daily walk should always be provided as this will appease his lively disposition. Care should always be taken not to overfeed as an overweight Miniature Dachshund can sometimes suffer with spinal trouble.

KEY TO CHARACTER	
INTELLIGENCE	***
TEMPERAMENT	****
EASE OF COAT CARE	
Smooth-haired	*****
Long-haired	***
Wire-haired	****
SUITABILITY FOR	*****
SMALL DWELLING	

***** (5) = VERY GOOD

BRITISH KENNEL CLUB STANDARD

DACHSHUND (Miniature Long-Haired)

CHARACTERISTICS. — The Miniature Dachshund should be gay, alert, bold and highly intelligent. Despite its small size it should be strong, extremely active, hardy and game. Movement should be free and gay. Both fore and hind feet should move straight forward without plaiting or crossing in front and free from any tendency to throw out the hind feet sideways.

GENERAL APPEARANCE. — In conformation the Miniature Dachshund should be in all respects similar to the Dachshund of standard size. It should be compact, short-legged and long in body, well muscled and strong, with bold and intelligent expression. The body should be neither so plump as to give an impression of cobbiness, nor so slender as to impart a weasel-like appearance. Height at shoulder should be half the length of the body measured from the breast bone to the base of the tail, and the girth of the chest double the height at the shoulder. The length of from the tip of the nose to the eyes should be equal the length from eyes to base of skull.

Head and Skull. — Long and conical when seen from above, sharp in profile and finely modelled. Skull neither too broad nor too narrow, only slightly arched and without prominent stop. Foreface long and narrow, finely modelled. The lips should be tightly drawn but well covering the lower jaw, neither heavy nor too sharply cut away. The corners of the mouth slightly marked.

Eyes. — Of medium size, neither prominent not too deeply set, oval in shape placed obliquely. They should be clear and expressive and dark in colour except in Dapples and Chocolates, in which wall or light eyes are permissible.

Ears. — Broad and placed relatively well back, high and well set on, lying close to the cheeks and very mobile. The leather of the ears when pulled to the front should not extend beyond the tip of the nose.

Mouth. — Wide, extending back to behind the eyes. Teeth sound and strong, the inner side of the upper incisors closing on the outer side of the under ones.

Smooth-Haired Dachshund
Wire-Haired Dachshund

Miniature Long-Haired Dachshund
Miniature Smooth-Haired Dachshund

Neck. — Long and muscular, showing do dewlap, slightly arched at the nape, running cleanly into the shoulders, carried well up, giving the dog an alert, defiant appearance.

Forequarters. — Muscular, with deep chest. Shoulder blades should be long and broad, set obliquely and lying firmly on well-developed ribs. The breast bone should be prominent, extending so far forward as to show depressions on both sides. Upper arm equal in length to the shoulder blade, which it should join at an angle of 90 degrees, well boned and muscled, set on close to the ribs but moving freely. Lower arm short, inclined slightly inwards, well boned and free from wrinkle.

Body. — Long and well muscled with oblique shoulders and short strong pelvic region. Ribs well-sprung and extending far back. Chest oval, well let down between the forelegs, with the deepest point of the keel level with the wrist-joints. The line of the back level or only slightly depressed over the shoulders and slightly arched over the loin, with the belly moderately tucked up.

Hindquarters. — Rump full, round and broad. Pelvis bone not too short, broad, strong and set obliquely. Thigh bone strong, of good length and jointed to the pelvis at an angle of 90 degrees. Second thighs short, set at right angles to the upper thigh and well muscled. Hocks well let down, set wide apart, strongly bent. Seen from behind the legs should be straight, with no tendency for the hocks to turn inwards or outwards.

Feet. — Broad and large in proportion to the size of the dog, straight or turned only slightly outwards. The hind feet smaller than the fore. Toes close together and with each toe well arched. Nails strong. The dog must stand equally on all parts of the foot.

Tail. — Set on fairly high, not too long, tapering and without too makred a curve. It should not be carried too high and never curled over the back.

Coat. — The coat should be soft and straight or only slightly waved. It is longest under the neck, on the under-parts of the body and behind the legs, where it should form abundant feathering and on the tail where it should form a flag. The outside of the ears should also be well feathered. The coat should be flat, resembling that of an Irish Setter, and should not obscure the outline. Too much hair on the feet is not desired.

Colour. — Any colour. No white is permissible except for a small spot on the breast and even this is undesirable. The nose should be black except in Dapples and Chocolates in which it may be flesh coloured or brown. In all cases the coat colour should be bright and clearly defined. In black and tans the tan should be rich and sharp. Dapples should be free from large unbroken patches, the dappling being evenly distributed over the whole body.

Weight and Size. — The ideal weight is 4.5Kg (10 lbs) and it is of the utmost importance that judges should not award a prize to any dog exceeding 5Kg (11 lbs) in weight. Other points being equal the smaller the better, but mere diminutiveness must never take precedence over general type and soundness. Any appearance of weediness or toyishness is to be avoided at all costs.

Faults. — Round skull. Round or protruding eyes. Short ears. Shallow chest. Narrowness in front or behind. Short body. Long legs. Splayed feet. Cow hocks. Mouth under or overshot. Nervous or cringing demeanour.

Note. — Male animals should have two apparently normal testicles fully descended into the scrotum.

MAIN AMERICAN KENNEL CLUB VARIATION TO THE STANDARD FOR MINIATURE LONG-HAIRED DACHSHUND —

Miniature Dachshunds have not been given separate classification but are a division of the Open Class for "under 10 pounds, and 12 months old or over".

DACHSHUND (Miniature Smooth-Haired)

The Standard of the Dachshund (Miniature Smooth-Haired) is identical with the Standard of the Dachshund (Miniature Long-Haired) with the following exceptions:-

Coat. — In Smooths, short, dense and smooth, adequately covering all the parts of the body; coarsest on the under-side of the tail.

Weight and Size. — The ideal weight is 4.5Kg (10 lbs) and it is of the utmost importance that judges should not award a prize to any dog exceeding 5Kg (11 lbs) in weight. Other points being equal the smaller the better, but mere diminutiveness must never take precedence over general type and soundness. Any appearance of weediness or toyishness is to be avoided at all costs.

Faults. — Wooly or curly coat.

MAIN AMERICAN KENNEL CLUB VARIATION TO THE STANDARD FOR MINIATURE SMOOTH-HAIRED DACHSHUND —

Miniature Dachshunds have not been given separate classification but are a division of the Open Class for "under 10 pounds, and 12 months old or over".

DACHSHUND (Miniature Wire-Haired)

The Standard of the Dachshund (Miniature Wire-Haired) is identical with the Standard of the Dachshund (Miniature Long-Haired) with the following exceptions:-

Coat. — With the exception of the jaw, eyebrows and ears, the whole body is covered with a completely even, short, harsh coat and undercoat. There should be a beard on the chin. The eyebrows are bushy. The hair on the ears is almost smooth.

Weight and Size. — The ideal weight is 4.5Kg (10 lbs) and it is of the utmost importance that judges should not award a prize to any dog exceeding 5Kg (11 lbs) in weight. Other points being equal the smaller the better, but mere diminutiveness must never take precedence over general type and soundness. Any appearance of weediness or toyishness is to be avoided at all costs.

MAIN AMERICAN KENNEL CLUB VARIATION TO THE STANDARD FOR MINIATURE WIRE-HAIRED DACHSHUND —

Miniature Dachshunds have not been given separate classification but are a division of the Open Class for "under 10 pounds, and 12 months old or over".

Miniature Wire-Haired Dachshund
Deerhound

Elkhound
Finnish Spitz

MINIATURE DACHSHUND REGISTRATIONS 1981 — 87 INCLUSIVE

	LONG-HAIRED	SMOOTH-HAIRED	WIRE-HAIRED
1981 —	1837	1010	602
1982 —	1618	909	556
1983 —	1670	839	593
1984 —	1568	851	557
1985 —	1616	915	614
1986 —	1417	819	595
1987 —	1372	760	598

NO MINIATURE DACHSHUND HAS YET WON CRUFTS BEST-IN-SHOW.

DEERHOUND

This, one of the speediest of breeds, was developed in Scotland for one particular purpose, namely hunting deer. Having obvious physical characteristics similar to a Greyhound, the Deerhound was ideally suited to the task. He covers the ground in enormous athletic strides and even the fleet-footed red deer can barely match his pace.

As well as having Greyhound ancestry, he is also related to the Irish Wolfhound, as is clearly seen in the similarity of coat.

He has been a dog much favoured by Scottish aristocracy, being very much at home on huge, rolling highland estates. When out hunting, the Deerhound would show great single minded agression toward his prey, but this behaviour was seen to vanish once in his master's home. In fact his manners are excellent and if well treated he will repay with extreme devotion and affection.

Although the breed naturally declined with the reduction in deer hunting, he is still highly prized by his loyal, if not huge, band of followers in Britain. The Deerhound has that rare combination of speed, strength and grace and to be seen at his best a good deal of his life should be spent outdoors running free.

If an owner's home is large and he can spare sufficient time for exercise, the Deerhound makes an impressive pet. He is sensitive without being neurotic and a strong attachment between dog and owner usually develops.

Greyhound
Ibizan Hound

Irish Wolfhound
Otterhound

KEY TO CHARACTER	
INTELLIGENCE	***
TEMPERAMENT	****
EASE OF COAT CARE	****
SUITABILITY FOR SMALL DWELLING	*
***** (5) = VERY GOOD	

BRITISH KENNEL CLUB STANDARD

DEERHOUND

Head and Skull. — The head should be broadest at the ears, tapering slightly to the eyes, with the muzzle tapering more decidedly to the nose. The muzzle should be pointed but the lips level. The head should be long, the skull rather flat than round, with a very slight rise over the eyes, but with nothing approaching a stop. The skull should be coated with moderately long hair, which is softer than the rest of the coat. The nose should be black (though in some blue-fawns the colour is blue) and slightly aquiline. In the lighter coloured dogs a black muzzle is preferred. There should be a good moustache or rather silky hair, and a fair beard.

Eyes. — The eyes should be dark; generally they are dark-brown or hazel. A very light eye is not liked. The eye is moderately full, with a soft look in repose, but a keen, far-away look when the dog is roused. The rims of the eyelids should be black.

Ears. — The ears should be set on high, and, in repose, folded back like the Greyhound's, though raised above the head in excitement without losing the fold, and even in some cases semi-erect. A prick ear is bad. A big thick ear hanging flat to the head, or heavily coated with long hair, is the worst of faults. The ear should be soft, glossy, and like a mouse's coat to the touch, and the smaller it is the better. It should have no long coat or long fringe, but there is often a silky silvery coat on the body of the ear and the tip. Whatever the general colour, the ears should be black or dark-coloured.

Mouth. — Teeth level.

Neck. — The neck should be long; that is, of the length that befits the Greyhound character of the dog. An over-long neck is not necessary or desirable, for the dog is not required to stoop to his work like a Greyhound, and it must be remembered that the mane, which every good specimen should have, detracts from the apparent length of neck. Moreover, a Deerhound requires a very strong neck to hold a stag. The nape of the neck should be very prominent where the head is set on, and the throat should be clean cut at the angle and prominent.

Forequarters. — The shoulders should be well sloped, the blades well back and not too much width between them. Loaded and straight shoulders are very bad faults. The forelegs should be straight, broad and flat, a good broad forearm and elbow being desirable.

Body. — The body and general formation is that of a Greyhound of larger size and bone. Chest deep rather than broad, but not too narrow and flat-sided. The loin well arched and dropping to the tail. A straight back is not desirable, this formation being unsuitable for going uphill, and very unsightly.

Hindquarters. — Drooping, and as broad and powerful as possible, the hips being set wide apart. The hind legs should be well bent at the stifle, with great length from the hip to the hock, which should be broad and flat.

Feet. — Should be close and compact, with well arranged toes. Nails strong.

Tail. — Should be long, thick at the root, tapering, and reaching to within about 1½ inches of the ground. When the dog is still, dropped perfectly straight down, or curved. When in motion, it should be curved when excited, in no case to be lifted out of the line of the back. It should be well-covered with hair; on the inside, thick and wiry; on the underside longer, and towards the end a slight fringe is not objectionable. A curl or ring tail is very undesirable.

Coat. — The hair on the body, neck and quarters should be harsh and wiry, and about three to four inches long; that on the head, breast and belly is much softer. There should be a slight hairy fringe on the inside of the fore and hind legs, but nothing approaching the "feather" of a Collie. The Deerhound should be a shaggy dog, but not over-coated. A woolly coat is bad. Some good strains have a mixture of silky coat with the hard, which is preferable to a woolly coat; but the proper coat is a thick, close-lying, ragged coat, harsh or crisp to the touch.

Colour. — Colour is much a matter of fancy. But there is no manner of doubt that the dark blue-grey is the most preferred because quality tends to follow this colour. Next comes the darker and lighter greys or brindles, the darkest being generally preferred. Yellow and sandy-red or red-fawn, especially with black points, i.e., ears and muzzles, are also in equal estimation, this being the colour of the oldest-known strains, the McNeil and Cheethill Menzies. White is condemned by all the old authorities, but a white chest and white toes, occurring as they do in a great many of the darkest-coloured dogs, are not so greatly objected to, but the less the better, as the Deerhound is a self-coloured dog. A white blaze on the head, or a white collar should be heavily penalised. In other cases, though passable, yet an attempt should be made to get rid of white markings. The less white the better, but a slight white tip to the stern occurs in the best strains.

Weight and Size. — Should be from 38.6Kg to 47.7Kg (85 to 105 lbs) in dogs and from 29.5 to 36.3Kg (65 to 80 lbs) in bitches. Height of dogs should not be less than 76cm (30") and bitches 71cm (28") at the shoulder, respectively.

Faults. — Thick ear hanging flat to the head, or heavily coated with long hair. Curl or ring tail. Light eye. Straight back. Cow hocks, weak pasterns, straight stifles, splay feet, woolly coat, loaded and straight shoulders, white markings.

Note. — Male animals should have two apparently normal testicles fully descended into the scrotum.

Pharaoh Hound
Rhodesian Ridgeback

Saluki

Whippet

MAIN AMERICAN KENNEL CLUB VARIATION TO THE STANDARD FOR DEERHOUND —

Known as the Scottish Deerhound in the U.S.A.

Height. — Height of Dogs — from 30 to 32 inches. Height of Bitches — from 28 inches upwards.

Weight. — From 85 to 110 pounds in dogs, and from 75 to 95 pounds in bitches.

DEERHOUND REGISTRATIONS 1981 — 87

1981 — 161
1982 — 193
1983 — 176
1984 — 185
1985 — 216
1986 — 205
1987 — 298

YET TO WIN CRUFTS BEST-IN-SHOW.

ELKHOUND

The Elkhound was once extensively used in packs for hunting in his native Norway. His principal prey was, as his name indicates, the huge Scandanavian Elk. These hunts were a perilous pursuit that required dogs of great strength and positive character. The Elkhounds would risk severe injury or death from the massive antlers of the Elk whilst cornering it for their masters to kill. Often the prevailing conditions during a hunt would be appalling, driving snow, bitter cold and dense forest all had to be dealt with. A Spitz-type dog with his roots in the Arctic Circle was the obvious choice for such work and the Elkhound is a Spitz family member.

The breed is now quite well known in the U.S.A., and Europe and has figured to a fair degree in the show world, where he exhibits great self-confidence and even temper.

Although the modern Elkhounds have less hunting aggression than their forefathers, they still retain their rugged physical characteristics. They have endless stamina, are solidly built, being neither leggy not squat and they never feel the cold. The fairly fierce appearance might discourage some people but if the Elkhound puppy is sensibly trained from the outset, he can be as reliable as any breed. He guards his owners home well and although he will happily sleep outdoors, he enjoys the family environment. He possesses great energy and alertness and will be happiest with an owner of a similarly active disposition who could exercise his dog extensively.

KEY TO CHARACTER	
INTELLIGENCE	****
TEMPERAMENT	****
EASE OF COAT CARE	****
SUITABILITY FOR SMALL DWELLING	*
***** (5) = VERY GOOD	

BRITISH KENNEL CLUB STANDARD

ELKHOUND

CHARACTERISTICS. — The Elkhound is a hardy sporting dog of Nordic type of a bold and virile nature, and has good scenting power. Its disposition should be friendly and intelligent, with great energy and independence of character, and without any sign of undue nervousness.

GENERAL APPEARANCE. — It has a compact and proportionately short body, a coat thick and abundant but not bristling, and prick ears; tail tightly curled over back.

Head and Skull. — Broad between the ears; the forehead and back of the head are slightly arched with a clearly marked but not large stop. Muzzle moderately long, broader at the base and gradually tapering — whether seen from above or from the side — but not pointed; bridge of the nose straight, jaw strong with lips tightly closed.

Eyes. — Not prominent, in colour brown and as dark as possible, giving a frank, fearless and friendly expression.

Ears. — Set high, firm and upstanding, height slightly greater than their width at the base, pointed and very mobile.

Mouth. — Jaw strong with lips tightly closed, teeth meeting in a scissor bite.

Gait. — Demonstrates agility and endurance; stride at the trot even and effortless, back remaining level; as the speed of the trot increases, front and rear legs converge equally in straight lines towards a centre line beneath the body.

Neck. — Of medium length, firm, muscular and well set up.

Forequarters. — Legs firm straight and powerful with good bone; elbows closely set on.

Body. — Short in the couplings; back, wide and straight from neck to stern; chest, wide and deep with well-rounded ribs; loins, muscular; stomach, very little drawn up.

Hindquarters. — Hind legs firm strong and powerful, a little but definite bend at stifle and hock, and straight when viewed from behind.

Feet. — Compact, oval in shape and not turned outwards; toes, tightly closed; toe nails, firm and strong.

Tail. — Set high, tightly curled over the back but not carried on either side; hair, thick and coarse.

Coat. — Thick, abundant, course and weather-resisting; short on the head and on the front of the legs; longest on the chest, neck, buttocks, behind the forelegs and on the underside of the tail. It is composed of a longish and coarse top coat, dark at the tips with a light-coloured, soft and woolly undercoat. About the neck and front of the chest the longer coat forms a sort of ruff which, with the pricked ears, the energetic eyes and the curled tail, gives the animal its unique and alert appearance.

Colour. — Grey, of various shades with black tips to the long outer coat; lighter on the chest, stomach, legs, and the underside of the tail. Any distinctive variation from the grey colour is most undesirable and too dark or too light colouring should be avoided. Pronounced markings on legs and feet are also not desirable.

Weight and Size. — For dogs, the ideal height at the shoulder should be 52cm (20½″) and for bitches 49cm (19½″). Weight approximately 23Kg (50 lbs) and 20Kg (43 lbs) respectively.

Note. — Male animals should have two apparently normal testicles fully descended into the scrotum.

MAIN AMERICAN KENNEL CLUB VARIATION TO THE STANDARD FOR ELKHOUND —

Known as the Norwegian Elkhound in the U.S.A.

Size. — Weight for dogs about 55 pounds; for bitches about 48 pounds.

ELKHOUND REGISTRATIONS 1981 — 87 INCLUSIVE

1981 — 151
1982 — 161
1983 — 142
1984 — 199
1985 — 178
1986 — 175
1987 — 146

YET TO WIN CRUFTS BEST-IN-SHOW.

FINNISH SPITZ

Like most countries at the top of the northern hemisphere, Finland has it's own particular Spitz — type dog. Although the Finnish Spitz has only been recognised for about a hundred years, it seems probable that similar dogs have existed in Finland for centuries. He has been used as an efficient hunting dog, being particularly suited to bird work. This is not surprising, as closely related breeds from Russia and Norway are fine hunters, too. Although one of the lighter Spitz breeds, he is well capable of the often horrendous weather of Finland. His dense coat provides perfect insulation and he is of a fearless, positive disposition.

He is not a dog that figures very greatly outside his homeland, although in Britain a following is growing steadily, many now being seen at larger dog shows. He is a particularly striking show dog, mainly due to his fabulous bright red colour.

Despite his rugged past, the Finnish Spitz is a marvellous dog for the home. He is might what be called a very well-rounded breed, being clean, attractive, intelligent and friendly. He guards with great vigour and enjoys the company of children. Plenty of exercise is essential for this tireless breed and although not absolutely vital, a rural life might be preferred.

KEY TO CHARACTER	
INTELLIGENCE	****
TEMPERAMENT	*****
EASE OF COAT CARE	****
SUITABILITY FOR SMALL DWELLING	***
***** (5) = VERY GOOD	

BRITISH KENNEL CLUB STANDARD

FINNISH SPITZ

CHARACTERISTICS. — The Finnish Spitz characteristics are eagerness to hunt, courage, tempered with caution, fidelity and intelligence.

GENERAL APPEARANCE. — The dog is considerably larger and carries more coat than the bitch. Bearing bold. The whole appearance, particularly eyes, ears and tail indicates liveliness.

Head. — Medium sized and clean cut. Longer than it is broad in the ratio of 7:4. Forehead slightly arched, stop pronounced. Muzzle narrow, seen from above and from the sides evenly tapering. Nose pitch black. Lips tightly closed and thin. Scissor bite.

Eyes. — Medium sized, lively, preferably dark. Almond shaped, with black rims, set slightly aslant, with outer corners tilted upwards.

Ears. — Small, cocked, sharply pointed. Fine in texture and mobile.

Neck. — Muscular, of medium length — in males it may appear to be shorter due to a dense ruff.

Forequarters. — Stong and straight.

Body. — Almost square in outline. Back straight and strong. Chest deep. Belly slightly drawn up.

Hindquarters. — Strong. Only moderate turn of stifle.

Feet. — Preferably round. Hind dewclaws are always removed. Removal of front dewclaws optional.

Tail. — Plumed, curves vigorously from its root in an arch, forward, downward and backward, then pressing down against the thigh, with its tip extending to the middle part of the thigh. Extended, the bone of the tail usually reaches to the hock joint.

Coat. — On head and front legs short and close, on the body and back of legs longish, semi-erect or erect, stiffer on the neck and back. Outer coat on shoulders considerably longer and coarser, particularly in males. On back of thighs and on tail hair should be longer and denser. No trimming is allowed, not even of whiskers. Undercoat short, soft and dense.

Colour. — On the back reddish-brown or red-gold, preferably bright. The hairs on inner sides of ears, cheeks, under the muzzle, on the breast, abdomen, behind the shoulders, inside the legs, back of thighs, underside of tail, of lighter shades. Undercoat is also a lighter colour, making the whole coat glow. White markings on toes and a narrow white stripe, not exceeding two centimetres in width, on the breast permitted. Black hairs on lips and sparse separate black-pointed hairs on back and tail are permitted, even desirable. Puppies may have a good many black hairs which decrease with age, black on the tail persisting longer.

Gait. — Light and springy, quick and graceful.

Weight and Size. — Height at withers and length of body in males 44 to 50cm (17" to 20"), in females 39 to 45cm (15½" to 18"). Approximate weight in males 14 to 16Kg (31 to 36 lbs), in females 10 to 13Kg (23 to 29 lbs).

Faults. — Any departure from the foregoing points should be considered a fault and the seriousness of the fault should be in exact proportion to its degree.

Note. — Male animals should have two apparently normal testicles fully descended into the scrotum.

FINNISH SPITZ REGISTRATIONS 1981 — 87 INCLUSIVE

1981 — 55
1982 — 65
1983 — 75
1984 — 74
1985 — 63
1986 — 71
1987 — 67

YET TO WIN CRUFTS BEST-IN-SHOW.

GREYHOUND

The Greyhound is one of the oldest known breeds. In a similar form he existed in the Middle East some 4,000 years ago. These dogs were highly prized by the Arab people of the time and were used for the hunting of gazelle and other speedy prey which no other domesticated animal could pursue. These very early specimens of the Greyhound family were thought to have had fairly long, wispy coats, perhaps resembling a Saluki. As these dogs spread throughout other countries, their coat gradually evolved to suit different climatic conditions. The coat of the Afghan Hound, a member of the Greyhound family, developed it's coat in this way.

Today's smooth coated Greyhound has been in Britain for many hundreds of years and has been much favoured by royalty for hunting and for it's dignified air as a companion.

With his deep chest, arched loins and immense muscular quarters, the Greyhound is ideally built for speed. Indeed, it has been with this constant thought in mind that breeders have developed the near perfect running machine of today. Greyhound racing is as popular as ever and no other dog can sustain such speed for so long a distance.

Although happier to be racing or engaged in similar demanding work, the Greyhound can make a friendly companion. If treated well, he will respond with affection but he must never be teased as he can be a little impatient. Due to his extensive exercise needs, he should not be taken as a pet without careful thought.

KEY TO CHARACTER	
INTELLIGENCE	***
TEMPERAMENT	***
EASE OF COAT CARE	*****
SUITABILITY FOR SMALL DWELLING	*
***** (5) = VERY GOOD	

BRITISH KENNEL CLUB STANDARD

GREYHOUND

CHARACTERISTICS. — They Greyhound possesses remarkable stamina and endurance, its straight through, long reaching movement enables it to cover ground at great speed.

GENERAL APPEARANCE. — The general appearance of the typical Greyhound is that of a strongly built, upstanding dog of generous proportions, muscular power and symmetrical formation, with a long head and neck, clean well-laid shoulders, deep chest, capacious body, arched loin, powerful quarters, sound legs and feet, and a suppleness of limb, which emphasize in a marked degree its distinctive type and quality.

Head and Skull. — Long, moderate width, flat skull, slight stop. Jaws, powerful and well chiselled.

Eyes. — Bright and intelligent — oval — set obliquely.

Ears. — Small, rose-shape of fine texture.

Mouth. — Teeth white and strong. The incisors of the upper jaw clipping those of the lower jaw.

Neck. — Long and muscular, elegantly arched, well let into the shoulders.

Forequarters. — Shoulders, oblique, well set back, muscular without being loaded, narrow and cleanly defined at the top. Forelegs, long and straight, bone of good substance and quality. Elbows, free and well set under the shoulders. Pasterns, moderate length, slightly sprung. Elbows, pasterns and toes should incline neither outwards nor inwards.

Body. — Chest, deep and capacious, providing adequate heart room. Ribs, deep, well sprung, and carried well back. Flanks well cut up. Back, rather long, broad and square. Loin, powerful, slightly arched.

Hindquarters. — Thighs and second thighs, wide and muscular, showing great propelling power. Stifles, well bent. Hocks, well let down, inclining neither outwards nor inwards. Body and hindquarters features should be of ample proportions and well coupled, enabling adequate ground to be covered when standing.

Feet. — Moderate length, with compact well-knuckled toes, strong pads.

Gait. — Straight, low reaching free stride enabling it to cover ground at great speed. Hind legs should come well under body giving great propulsion.

Tail. — Long, set on rather low, strong at the root, tapering to the point, carried low, slightly curved.

Coat. — Fine and close.

Colour. — Black, white, red, blue, fawn, fallow, brindle, or any of the colours broken with white.

Height. — Ideal height: Dogs, 71 to 76cm (28″ to 30″); Bitches, 68 to 71cm (27″ to 28″).

Note. — Male animals should have two apparently normal testicles fully descended into the scrotum.

MAIN AMERICAN KENNEL CLUB VARIATION TO THE STANDARD FOR GREYHOUND —

Weight. — Dogs, 65 to 70 pounds; Bitches, 60 to 65 pounds.

GREYHOUND REGISTRATIONS 1981 — 87 INCLUSIVE

1981 — 57
1982 — 75
1983 — 40
1984 — 41
1985 — 83
1986 — 41
1987 — 68

CRUFTS BEST-IN-SHOW WINNER 3 TIMES.

1928 PRIMELEY SCEPTRE — H. WHITLEY
1934 SOUTHBALL MOONSTONE — B. HARTLAND WORDEN
1956 TREETOPS GOLDEN FALCON — MRS. W. DE CASEMBROOT and
MISS H. GREENISH

IBIZAN HOUND

The Ibizan Hound can lay claim to being one of the oldest of all breeds. Paintings and carvings in the tombs of the Egyptian Pharoahs have shown dogs bearing an extreme likeness to the Ibizan Hound, some dating back over, 5,000 years.

Having enjoyed a place of great importance with the Egyptians, it was around the eighth century that traders took specimens of these dogs with them to the Mediterranean and the island which lends the breed it's name, Ibiza.

Due to it's isolation, food was not always easily obtainable on Ibiza and the islanders quickly realised the potential of these new dogs for hunting small game. They used the dog's great speed in the pursuit of rabbit, hare and civet cat, which doubtless improved the quality of their diet. On the Spanish mainland too, the Ibizan Hound became evident and there it was hunted in packs for game as large as deer.

This breed has remained virtually unchanged since his distant beginnings and it is of great credit to modern breeders that they have resisted any temptation to alter him. Although the best dogs are still to be found on Ibiza, there are many excellent specimens all over the world.

As a pet he does have one or two drawbacks but if correctly managed he makes an imposing companion of great intelligence. Being built for running and jumping, large amounts of exercise are essential. He can be a little aloof but once attached to a family he will show great loyalty and affection towards them.

```
┌─────────────────────────────────────────────────┐
│              KEY TO CHARACTER                    │
├─────────────────────────────────────────────────┤
│   INTELLIGENCE              ****                  │
│                                                  │
│   TEMPERAMENT               ***                   │
│                                                  │
│   EASE OF COAT CARE         *****                 │
│                                                  │
│   SUITABILITY FOR           *                     │
│   SMALL DWELLING                                 │
├─────────────────────────────────────────────────┤
│           ***** (5) = VERY GOOD                  │
└─────────────────────────────────────────────────┘
```

BRITISH KENNEL CLUB STANDARD

INTERIM STANDARD OF THE IBIZAN HOUND

CHARACTERISTICS. — A tireless controlled hunter. Retrieves to hand, very kind, rather cautious with strangers, has the ability to jump great heights without take-off run. An agile hound.

GENERAL APPEARANCE. — Tall, narrow, finely built, large erect ears.

Head and Skull. — Fine, long flat skull with prominent occipital bone. Stop not well defined, slightly convex muzzle, the length of which from the eyes to the tip of the nose should be equal to the length from the eyes to the occiput. Nose flesh coloured, should protrude beyond the teeth, jaw very strong and lean.

Eyes. — Clear amber, expressive. Almond shaped; not prominent, large or round.

Ears. — Large, thin, stiff, highly mobile, erect when dog is alert, in a continuous line with the arch of the neck when viewed in profile; base set on level with the eyes.

Mouth. — Perfectly even white teeth; scissor bite; thin lips with no dew-lap.

Neck. — Very lean, long, muscular and slightly arched.

Forequarters. — Rather steep short shoulder blade, long straight legs, erect pasterns of good length.

Body. — Level back sloping slightly from the pinbones to the rump. Long, flat ribcage. Short coupled with well tucked up waist, breast bone very prominent. Depth measured between the bottom of the ribcage and elbow 2½ inches to 3 inches.

Hindquarters. — Long, strong, straight and lean, no great angulation, long second thigh, turning neither in nor out.

Feet. — Well arched toes, thick pads, light coloured claws. Front feet may turn slightly outwards. Dew claws should not be removed in front. No hind dew claws.

Gait. — A suspended trot, which is a long far reaching stride, with a slight hover before placing the foot to the ground.

Tail. — Long, thin, low set, reaching well below the hock, when passed between the legs and round the flank should reach the spine; may be carried high when excited but not curled within itself or low over the back.

Coat. — Either smooth or rough always hard, close, dense. Longer under the tail and at the back of the legs. Hunting scars should not be penalised.

Colour. — White, Chestnut, or Lion solid colour, or any combination of these.

Weight and Size. — The Standard in the country of origin varies between 56 and 74cm (22″ to 29″), but balance is the overriding factor.

Faults. — Any departure from the foregoing, the degree of the departure stipulating the seriousness of the fault.

Note. — Male animals should have two apparently normal testicles fully descended into the scrotum.

MAIN AMERICAN KENNEL CLUB VARIATION TO THE STANDARD FOR IBIZAN HOUND —

Height. — Height of dogs at withers ranges from 23½ to 27½ inches; height of bitches at withers ranges from 22½ to 26 inches.

Weight. — Average weight of dogs, 50 pounds; Bitches, 42 to 49 pounds.

IBIZAN HOUND REGISTRATIONS 1981 — 87 INCLUSIVE

1981 — 15
1982 — 25
1983 — 16
1984 — 38
1985 — 14
1986 — 25
1987 — 37

YET TO WIN CRUFTS BEST-IN-SHOW.

IRISH WOLFHOUND

This is the true canine giant, the world's tallest dog. Despite his size he is neither lumbering nor clumsy, moving with grace and controlled power. His elegance and pleasing proportions can be largely attributed to the efforts of a certain Captain George Graham who spent over twenty years perfecting the standard, concluding his work in 1885.

As is plain to see, there is a good deal of Deerhound in the Irish Wolfhound's blood and some of the other breeds used by Captain Graham were of Great Dane descent.

The very early version of the breed was of lighter build and was referred to as the Irish Greyhound, being very similar to the Deerhound of today. They were used, in Ireland, to hunt deer, wolves and elk. When this type of prey diminished, so the breed declined. It was from here on that Captain Graham's efforts came to the rescue.

Today's Wolfhound has an excellent genial nature and makes a first class companion, if you have sufficient space for him. He is level headed and loyal, making an intimidating guard when roused.

KEY TO CHARACTER	
INTELLIGENCE	****
TEMPERAMENT	*****
EASE OF COAT CARE	***
SUITABILITY FOR SMALL DWELLING	*
***** (5) = VERY GOOD	

BRITISH KENNEL CLUB STANDARD

IRISH WOLFHOUND

GENERAL APPEARANCE. — The Irish Wolfhound should not be quite so heavy or massive as the Great Dane, but more so than the Deerhound, which in general type he should otherwise resemble. Of great size and commanding appearance, very muscular, strongly though gracefully built, movements easy and active; head and neck carried high; the tail carried with an upward sweep with a slight curve towards the extremity.

Head and Skull. — Long, the frontal bones of the forehead very slightly raised and very little indentaiton between the eyes. Skull, not too broad. Muzzle, long and moderately pointed.

Eyes. — Dark.

Ears. — Small and Greyhound-like in carriage.

Neck. — Rather long, very strong and muscular, well arched, without dewlap or loose skin about the throat.

Forequarters. — Shoulders muscular, giving breadth of chest, set sloping. Elbows well under, turned neither inwards nor outwards. Leg and forearm muscular, and the whole leg strong and quite straight.

Body. — Chest, very deep. Breast, wide. Back, rather long than short. Loins arched. Belly well drawn up.

Hindquarters. — Muscular thighs and second thighs; long and strong as in the Greyhound, and hocks well let down and turning neither in nor out.

Feet. — Moderately large and round, turned neither inwards nor outwards. Toes well arched and closed. Nails very strong and curved.

Tail. — Long and slightly curved, of moderate thickness, and well covered with hair.

Coat. — Rough and hardy on body, legs and head; especially wiry and long over eyes and under jaw.

Colour. — The recognised colours are grey, brindle, red, black, pure white, fawn, or any colour that appears in the Deerhound.

Weight and Size. — The minimum height and weight of dogs should be 79cm (31") and 54.5Kg (120 lbs); of bitches, 71cm (28") and 40.9Kg (90 lbs). *Anything below this should be heavily penalised.* Great size, including height at shoulder and proportionate length of body, is the desideratum to be aimed at, and it is desired to firmly establish a breed that shall average from 81 to 86cm (32" to 34") in dogs, showing the requisite power, activity, courage and symmetry.

Faults. — Too light or heavy a head, too highly arched frontal bone; large ears; ears hanging flat to the face; short neck; full dewlap; too narrow or too broad a chest; sunken, hollow or quite straight back; bent forelegs; overbent fetlocks; twisted feet; spreading toes; too curly a tail; weak hind-quarters and a general want of muscle; too short in body; pink or liver-coloured eyelids; lips and nose any colour other than black; very light eyes.

Note. — Male animals should have two apparently normal testicles fully descended into the scrotum.

MAIN AMERICAN KENNEL CLUB VARIATION TO THE STANDARD FOR IRISH WOLFHOUND —

General Appearance. — The minimum height and weight of dogs should be 32 inches and 120 pounds; of bitches, 30 inches and 105 pounds.

IRISH WOLFHOUND REGISTRATIONS 1981 — 87 INCLUSIVE

1981 — 623
1982 — 618
1983 — 686
1984 — 645
1985 — 700
1986 — 719
1987 — 646

CRUFTS BEST-IN-SHOW WINNER 1960

SULHAMSTEAD MERMAN — MRS NAGLE AND MISS CLARK

OTTERHOUND

This is a rare and ancient breed and one of the finest hunting dogs ever developed. Although he was undoubtedly perfected in Britain for the sole purpose of otter hunting, his early ancesty is open to question. Some believe his origins to be British and that his main ancestor was the Southern Hound, a long-extinct hunting dog. There is strong support, though, for the view that his roots are in France and that he comes from the same stock as the Basset Griffon Vendeen, a shaggy coated Basset Hound-type. There is also a resemblance to the Bloodhound in the Otterhound's bone structure, so this is another possibility.

For centuries the sport of otter hunting was widespread among the upper classes of Britain and they succeeded in developing the perfect dog for this demanding form of hunting. He has a waterproof coat and excellent swimming ability, partly due to his feet actually being webbed. He has a fine nose and is renowned for strength and stamina.

It is now illegal to hunt otters so the breed has been perpetuated purely by those who are interested in the undoubted beauty and character of these dogs. Although life in an average home would be difficult for the Otterhound, he does show great affection towards people and is excellent with children. Anyone contemplating owning an Otterhound will need plenty of space and must have the time to give his dog lengthy outings. A rural environment is virtually essential for this rugged breed.

```
┌─────────────────────────────────────────────────────┐
│                 KEY TO CHARACTER                      │
├─────────────────────────────────────────────────────┤
│                                                       │
│   INTELLIGENCE                    ****                │
│                                                       │
│   TEMPERAMENT                     ****                │
│                                                       │
│   EASE OF COAT CARE               ***                 │
│                                                       │
│   SUITABILITY FOR                  *                  │
│   SMALL DWELLING                                      │
├─────────────────────────────────────────────────────┤
│              ***** (5) = VERY GOOD                    │
└─────────────────────────────────────────────────────┘
```

BRITISH KENNEL CLUB STANDARD

INTERIM STANDARD FOR THE OTTERHOUND

CHARACTERISTICS. — An amiable, even tempered hound.

GENERAL APPEARANCE. — A big strongly built hound, straight limbed and sound, rough-coated with majestic head, strong body and loose long-striding action. Being primarily built for a long day's work in water, the rough double coat and large feet are essential. As the hound must be able to gallop on land, it must be free moving.

Head and Skull. — Clean and very imposing, deep rather than wide, clean cheekbones, skull nicely domed, not coarse nor overdone, rising from a distinct though not exaggerated stop to slight peak at the occiput. There should be no trace of scowl or bulge in forehead, the expression being open and amiable. Muzzle strong and deep with good wide nose ending in wide nostrils. Distance from nose-end to stop slightly shorter than from stop to occiput. Plenty of lip and flew, but not exaggerated. The whole head, except for nose should be well covered with rough hair, ending in slight moustaches and beard, both being part of the natural face hair.

Eyes. — An intelligent, moderately deepset eye, the haw showing only slightly. Eye colour and rim pigment variable according to coat colour, e.g. a blue and tan hound may have hazel eyes. Yellow eye undesirable.

Ears. — A unique feature of the breed. Should be long and pendulous, set on a level with the corner of the eye, easily reaching the nose when pulled forward, with the characteristic fold which denotes pure breeding. The leading edge should fold or roll inwards giving a curious, draped appearance. This is an essential point, which should not be lost. Well covered and fringed with hair.

Mouth. — Strong, very large, well placed teeth with scissor bite; viz. the jaws should be strong, with a perfect regular and complete scissor bite, i.e. the upper teeth closely overlapping the lower teeth and set square to the jaws. Level bite permissible.

Neck. — Neck long and powerful, set smoothly into well laid back, clean shoulders. Slight dew lap permissible.

Forequarters. — Forelegs strongly boned, straight from elbow to ground. Pasterns strong and slightly sprung.

Body. — Chest deep with well sprung oval ribcage which should be fairly long, with ribs carried well back allowing for plenty of heart and lung room; neither too wide nor too narrow. Body very strong with level top line and broad back. Loin short and strong. Angulation both at shoulder and elbow.

Hindquarters. — Very strong and well muscled when viewed from any angle, standing neigher too wide nor too narrow behind. The stifle fairly well bent; hocks well let down, turning neither in nor out. Thighs and second thighs heavily muscled. In natural stance, the hind legs from the hock to the ground should be perpendicular.

Feet. — Feet large, round, well knuckled, thick padded, turning neither in nor out. Compact when standing but capable of spreading, the hind feet only slightly smaller than the fore-feet. Web must be in evidence.

Gait. — Peculiar to the Otterhound, gait very loose and shambling at a walk, springing immediately into a loose and very long-striding sound, active trot. The gallop smooth and exceptionally long-striding.

Tail. — Set high and carried up when alert or on the move, it should never curl over the back and may droop when standing. Thick at the base, tapering to a point; bone should reach to the hock and be carried straight or in a slight curve. The hair under the tail (stern) rather longer and more profuse than that on the upper surface.

Coat. — Should be long (4 to 8cm; 1½″ to 3″) dense, rough, harsh and waterproof. An undercoat should be evident and there may be a slightly oily texture both in top and undercoat. The Otterhound requires no trimming for exhibition. Presentation should be natural.

Colour. — Recognised hound colours permissible:— Whole coloured, grizzle, sandy, red, wheaten, blue; these may have slight white markings on head, chest, feet and tail tip. White hounds may have slight lemon, blue or badger pied markings. Black and tan, blue and tan, black and tan, black and cream, occasional liver, tan and liver, tan and white. Colours not permissible:— Liver and white, a white bodied hound with black and tan patches distincly separate. Pigment should harmonize though not necessarily blend with coat colour; for example a tan hound may have a brown nose and eye rims. A slight butterfly nose is permissible.

Size. — Dogs approximately 67cm (27″) at the shoulder. Bitches approximately 60cm (24″) at the shoulder.

Faults. — Any departure from the foregoing points should be considered a fault and the seriousness with which the fault should be regarded should be in exact proportion to its degree.

Note. — Male animals should have two apparently normal testicles fully descended into the scrotum.

MAIN AMERICAN KENNEL CLUB VARIATION TO THE STANDARD FOR OTTERHOUND —

Size. — Males range from 24 to 27 inches at the withers, and weigh from 75 to 115 pounds, depending on the height and condition of the hound. Bitches are 22 to 26 inches at the withers and 65 to 100 pounds.

OTTERHOUND REGISTRATIONS 1981 — 87 INCLUSIVE

1981 — 52
1982 — 44
1983 — 35
1984 — 43
1985 — 34
1986 — 64
1987 — 34

YET TO WIN CRUFTS BEST-IN-SHOW.

PHARAOH HOUND

Some contend that this is the oldest known domesticated dog, this argument being supported by the many drawings of similar dogs that have been found in and around Egyptian burial places. In fact there have been discoveries of mummified dogs that were also of comparable type to the Pharaoh Hound. But the most likely explanation seems to be that these dogs were the progenitors of all the Greyhound-type dogs of the world, the Pharaoh Hound certainly being one such breed.

The Egyptians had prized their dogs as great hunters, and eventually travellers from Europe also saw their potential and began to take specimens home with them. It was over 2,000 years ago when the Mediterranean regions began to see these dogs in any quantity. Some reached the Balearic Islands particularly Ibiza and Malta. The Ibizan Hound of today descends from this early stock and Malta became the place of the Pharaoh Hound's development. The Maltese used the great speed and surprisingly keen nose of the breed for the hunting of small game and he is known there as 'Kelb-tal-fenek' which translates to 'rabbit-dog'.

This is a fairly new breed to Britain but already he is to be seen in good numbers at the major dog shows. His glorious tan coat always creates a stir and he is usually steady and well-behaved in the ring.

The Pharaoh Hound would not be a good choice for every home, because there is still a lot of the hunter in his make-up. But he has an amiable disposition and will remain loyal and affectionate if given plenty of exercise every day.

KEY TO CHARACTER	
INTELLIGENCE	****
TEMPERAMENT	****
EASE OF COAT CARE	*****
SUITABILITY FOR SMALL DWELLING	*
***** (5) = VERY GOOD	

BRITISH KENNEL CLUB STANDARD

PHARAOH HOUND

CHARACTERISTICS. — An intelligent, friendly, affectionate, playful and alert breed. An alert keen hunter, the Pharaoh Hound hunts by scent and sight using its large ears to a marked degree when working close.

GENERAL APPEARANCE. — The Pharaoh Hound is medium sized, of noble bearing with clean-cut lines. Graceful yet powerful. Very fast with free easy movement and alert expression.

Head and Skull. — Skull long, lean and well-chiselled. Foreface slightly longer than the skull. Only slight stop. Top of skull parallel with the foreface, the whole head representing a blunt wedge when viewed in profile and from above.

Eyes. — Amber coloured, blending with the coat; oval, moderately deep set with keen, intelligent expression.

Ears. — Medium high set; carried erect when alert, but very mobile; broad at the base, fine and large.

Mouth. — Powerful jaws with strong teeth. Scissor bite.

Nose. — Flesh coloured only, blending with the coat.

Neck. — Long, lean, muscular and slightly arched. Clean throat line.

Forequaters. — *Shoulders* — Strong, long and well laid back. *Forelegs* — Straight and parallel. Elbows well tucked in. Pasterns strong.

Body. — Lithe with almost straight topline. Slight slope down from croup to root of tail. Deep brisket extending down to point of elbow. Ribs well sprung. Moderate cut up. Length of body from breast to haunch bone slightly longer than height at withers.

Hindquarters. — Strong and muscular. Moderate bend of stifle. Well developed second thigh. Limbs parallel when viewed from behind.

Feet. — Strong, well knuckled and firm, turning neither in nor out. Paws well padded. Dew claws may be removed.

Gait. — Free and flowing; the head should be held fairly high and the dog should cover the ground well without any apparent effort. The legs and feet should move in line with the body; any tendency to throw the feet sideways, or a high stepping "hackney" action is a definite fault.

Tail. — Medium set — fairly thick at the base and tapering (whip-like), reaching just below the point of hock in repose. Carried high and curved when the dog is in action. The tail should not be tucked between the legs. A screw tail is a fault.

Coat. — Short and glossy, ranging from fine and close to slightly harsh; no feathering.

Colour. — Tan or rich tan with white markings allowed as follows:-
White tip on tail strongly desired.
White on chest (called "The Star").
White on toes.
Slim white blaze on centre line of face permissible.
Flecking or white other than above undesirable.

Height. — Dogs; Ideally 56 to 63cm (22″ to 25″). Bitches; Ideally 53 to 61cm (21″ to 24″). Overall balance must be maintained.

Faults. — Any deviation from the foregoing is a fault, hunting blemishes excepted.

Note. — Male animals should have two apparently normal testicles fully descended into the scrotum.

MAIN AMERICAN KENNEL CLUB VARIATION TO THE STANDARD FOR PHARAOH HOUND —

Height. — Dogs 23 inches to 25 inches. Bitches 21 inches to 24 inches.

PHARAOH HOUND REGISTRATIONS 1981 — 87 INCLUSIVE

1981 — 36
1982 — 24
1983 — 23
1984 — 25
1985 — 35
1986 — 81
1987 — 121

YET TO WIN CRUFTS BEST-IN-SHOW.

RHODESIAN RIDGEBACK

A ridge-backed hunting dog has existed in South Africa for hundreds of years. The ridge on the back is a tapering strip of backward-growing hair and all the finest hunting dogs were seen to possess it. Amazing as it may seem, South African tribesmen would use these dogs for lion hunting. The technique seems to have been for a pack of the dogs to torment and entice the lion out into the open where he could be slain. The agility and courage of these dogs must have been phenomenal and although the dogs we know today have been slightly 'watered-down' by European canine blood, the Rhodesian Ridgeback still possesses great strength and self-confidence.

As well as his hunting prowess, the Rhodesian Ridgeback has a history of guarding his owner and his property with great ferocity. This side to his character only appears in the required situation and in the home he is gentle and affectionate with the whole family.

He is a dog of good intelligence, learning easily which is a definite asset when training such a powerful dog. Someone with a good size house and garden would be preferred as an owner and to keep the Rhodesian Ridgeback's taut muscularity, a large amount of regular exercise is needed.

It would be hoped that nobody would purchase one of these fine dogs on a whim, purely for the novelty of the unique coat.

KEY TO CHARACTER	
INTELLIGENCE	****
TEMPERAMENT	****
EASE OF COAT CARE	*****
SUITABILITY FOR SMALL DWELLING	*
***** (5) = VERY GOOD	

BRITISH KENNEL CLUB STANDARD

RHODESIAN RIDGEBACK

CHARACTERISTICS. — The peculiarity of the breed is the ridge on the back which is formed by the hair growing in the opposite direction to the rest of the coat; the ridge must be regarded as the escutcheon of the breed. The ridge must be clearly defined, tapering and symmetrical. It must start immediately behind the shoulders and continue up to the hip (haunch) bones, and must contain two identical crowns only opposite each other. The lower edges of the crowns must not extend further down the ridge than one-third of the length of the ridge. Up to two inches is a good average for the width of the ridge.

GENERAL APPEARANCE. — The Ridgeback should represent a strong, muscular and active dog, symmetrical in outline, and capable of great endurance with a fair amount of speed. Movement should be similar to the Foxhound's gait.

Head and Skull. — Should be of fair length, the skull flat and rather broad between the ears and should be free from wrinkles when in repose. The stop should be reasonably well defined, and not in one straight line from the nose to the occiput bone as required in a Bull Terrier. The nose should be black or brown, in keeping with the colour of the dog. No other coloured nose is permissible. A black nose should be accompanied by dark eyes; a brown nose by amber eyes.

Eyes. — Should be moderately well apart, and should be round, bright and sparkling, with intelligent expression, their colour harmonising with the colour of the dog.

Ears. — Should be set up rather high, of medium size, rather wide at base, and gradually tapering to a rounded point. They should be carried close to the head.

Mouth. — The muzzle should be long, deep and powerful, jaws level and strong, with well developed teeth, especially the canines or holders. The lips should be clean, closely fitting the jaws.

Neck. — Should be fairly long, strong and free from throatiness.

Forequarters. — The shoulders should be sloping, clean and muscular, denoting speed. The forelegs should be perfectly straight, strong and heavy in bone; elbows close to the body.

Body. — The chest should not be too wide but very deep and capacious; ribs moderately well sprung, never rounded like barrel-hoops (which would indicate want of speed). The back powerful, and loins strong, muscular and slightly arched.

Hindquarters. — In the hind legs the muscles should be clean, well defined and hocks well down.

Feet. — The feet should be compact with well arched toes, round, tough elastic pads, protected by hair between the toes and pads.

Gait. — Straight forward movement, free and active.

Tail. — Should be strong at the insertion and generally tapering towards the end, free from coarseness. It should not be inserted too high or too low, and should be carried with a slight curve upwards, never curled.

Coat. — Should be short and dense, sleek and glossy in appearance but neither woolly nor silky.

Colour. — Light wheaten to red wheaten. Head, body, legs and tail should be of a uniform colour. A litle white on the chest is permissible but excessive white hairs here, on belly, or above paws should be penalised. White toes are undesirable. Dark muzzle and ears are permissible.

Weight and Size. — The desirable weight is dogs 36.3Kg (80 lbs) and bitches 31.7Kg (70 lbs) with a permissible variation of 2.2Kg (5 lbs) above and below these weights. A mature Ridgeback should be a handsome upstanding dog; dogs should be of a height of 63 to 68cm (25″ to 27″) and bitches 61 to 66cm (24″ to 26″). Minimum bench standard; dogs 63cm (25″) and bitches 61cm (24″).

Note. — Male animals should have two apparently normal testicles fully descended into the scrotum.

MAIN AMERICAN KENNEL CLUB VARIATION TO THE STANDARD FOR RHODESIAN RIDGEBACK —

Weight. — (Desirable) dogs 75 pounds, bitches 65 pounds.

RHODESIAN RIDGEBACK REGISTRATIONS 1981 — 87 INCLUSIVE

1981 — 366
1982 — 351
1983 — 441
1984 — 507
1985 — 636
1986 — 623
1987 — 709

YET TO WIN CRUFTS BEST-IN-SHOW.

SALUKI

The elegant Saluki is a member of the most ancient family of dogs, the Greyhounds with an ancestry dating possibly from 8,000 B.C. Carvings and drawings from the age of the Egyptian Pharaohs have shown Greyhound-type dogs, some resembling Salukis and even mummified specimens have been unearthed in tombs.

Sometimes known as the Gazelle Hound, the Saluki has always been used for hunting in the Middle East. He is a sighthound, that is, he depends more on his eyes than on his nose to detect his prey which, as his name suggests, is normally gazelle. He was a natural choice for this kind of hunting as no other dog could match the gazelle for speed and he had the necessary strength to bring down his quarry. So great was the hunting prowess of the Saluki that he was held in almost God-like reverance by the people of the Middle East, particularly among nomadic tribesmen who depended on game hunting to survive. The Saluki is still used to hunt gazelle, although to a lesser extent and he is still much-loved in his homeland.

If a prospective owner is prepared to give his dog a great deal of vigorous exercise and has a good-sized home, the Saluki could be for him. He enjoys the company of children although such an aristocratic breed does not like too much teasing. He guards well and will become intensely loyal to his owner and wary of strangers.

KEY TO CHARACTER	
INTELLIGENCE	****
TEMPERAMENT	****
EASE OF COAT CARE	*****
SUITABILITY FOR SMALL DWELLING	*
***** (5) = VERY GOOD	

BRITISH KENNEL CLUB STANDARD

SALUKI OR GAZELLE HOUND

GENERAL APPEARANCE. — The whole appearance of this breed should give an impression of grace and symmetry and of great speed and endurance coupled with strength and activity to enable it to kill gazelle or other quarry over deep sand or rocky mountain. The expression should be dignified and gentle with deep, faithful, farseeing eyes.

Head and Skull. — Head long and narrow; skull moderately wide between ears, not domed, the stop not pronounced, the whole showing great quality. Nose black or liver.

Eyes. — Dark to hazel and bright, large and oval, but not prominent.

Ears. — Long and mobile, covered with long silky hair; hanging close to the skull.

Mouth. — Teeth strong and level.

Neck. — Long, supple and well muscled.

Forequarters. — Shoulders sloping and set well back, well muscled without being coarse. The chest deep and moderately narrow. The forelegs straight and long from the elbow to the knee.

Body. — Back fairly broad, muscles slightly arched over the loin.

Hindquarters. — Strong, hip bones set wide apart, and stifle moderately bent, hocks low to the ground, showing galloping and jumping power.

Feet. — Of moderate length, toes long, and well arched, not splayed out, but at the same time not cat footed; the whole being strong and supple and well feathered between the toes.

Tail. — Long, set on low and carried naturally in a curve, well feathered on the underside with long silky hair, not bushy.

Coat. — Smooth and of a soft silky texture; slight feather on the legs; feather at the back of the thighs; sometimes with slight woolly feather on thigh and shoulders. (In the Smooth variety the points should be the same with the exception of the coat which has no feathering).

Colour. — White, cream, fawn, golden, red, grizzle and tan, tricolour (white, black and tan), and black and tan, or variations of these colours.

Weight and Size. — Height should average 58 to 71cm (23" to 28"), bitches proportionately smaller.

Note. — Male animals should have two apparently normal testicles fully descended into the scrotum.

SALUKI REGISTRATIONS 1981 — 87 INCLUSIVE

1981 — 272
1982 — 182
1983 — 184
1984 — 168
1985 — 213
1986 — 178
1987 — 118

YET TO WIN CRUFTS BEST-IN-SHOW.

WHIPPET

There is some controversy concerning the exact beginnings of the Whippet, although it seems indisputable that the Greyhound and/or the Italian Greyhound have played a major part in his origination.

For more than a century, Whippet racing has been a popular sport and in the early days it was more widespead than Greyhound racing. It is thought that some of these fanatical racing men of Englands northern counties crossed some of their dogs with various terriers. This was hoped to increase the dog's courage and hardiness but, most probably, decreased his pace. No Whippet litters of today ever throw up any terrier-like specimens which probably shows that these out crossings were few and far between. In fact, the Whippet has probably bred true to type for several centuries.

Obviously the most widely known attribute of this breed is his speed, which can exceed 40 m.p.h. Straight track racing and coursing take full advantage of this prodigious asset. But as a companion and house dog the Whippet has much to offer. He is exceptionally clean, inexpensive to feed and splendidly behaved with children. He is far hardier than he appears but in the winter care should be taken to protect him from extremes of cold. Exercise should be very frequent and lengthy but the Whippet will live happily in a small house or flat.

```
┌─────────────────────────────────────────────────────────┐
│                   KEY TO CHARACTER                      │
├─────────────────────────────────────────────────────────┤
│                                                         │
│   INTELLIGENCE                         ***              │
│                                                         │
│   TEMPERAMENT                          ***              │
│                                                         │
│   EASE OF COAT CARE                    *****            │
│                                                         │
│   SUITABILITY FOR                      ****             │
│   SMALL DWELLING                                        │
│                                                         │
├─────────────────────────────────────────────────────────┤
│              ***** (5) = VERY GOOD                      │
└─────────────────────────────────────────────────────────┘
```

BRITISH KENNEL CLUB STANDARD

WHIPPET

GENERAL APPEARANCE. — Should convey an impresson of beautifully balanced muscular power and strength, combined with great elegance and grace of outline. Symmetry of outline, muscular development and powerful gait are the main considerations; the dog being built for speed and work all forms of exaggeration should be avoided. The dog should possess great freedom of action, the forelegs should be thrown forward and low over the ground like a thoroughbred horse not in a Hackney-like action. Hind legs should come well under the body giving great propelling power, general movement not to look stilted, high stepping or in a short or mincing manner.

Head and Skull. — Long and lean, flat on top tapering to the muzzle, rather wide between the eyes, the jaws powerful and clean cut, nose black, in blues a bluish colour is permitted and in livers a nose of the same colour and in whites or parti-colour a butterfly nose is permissible.

Eyes. — Bright, expression very alert.

Ears. — Rose-shaped, small and fine in texture.

Mouth. — Level. The teeth in the top jaw fitted closely over the teeth in lower jaw.

Neck. — Long and muscular, elegantly arched.

Forequarters. — Shoulders oblique and muscular the blades carried up to the spine closely set together at the top. Forelegs straight and upright, front not too wide, pasterns strong with slight spring, elbows well set under the body.

Body. — Chest very deep with plenty of heart-room, brisket deep and well defined, brack back, firm, somewhat long and showing definite arch over the loin but not humped, loin giving the impression of strength and power, ribs well sprung; well muscled on back.

Hindquarters. — Strong and broad across thighs, stifles well bent, hocks well let down, second thighs strong, the dog then being able to stand over a lot of ground and show great driving power.

Feet. — Very neat, well split up between the toes, knuckles highly arched, pads thick and strong.

Tail. — No feathering. Long, tapering, when in action carried in a delicate curve upward but not over the back.

Coat. — Fine, short, as close as possible in texture.

Colour. — Any colour or mixture of colours.

Weight and Size. — The ideal height for dogs is 47cm (18½″) and for bitches 44cm (17½″). Judges should use their discretion and not unduly penalise an otherwise good specimen.

Faults. — FRONT AND SHOULDERS — Weak, sloping or too straight pasterns, pigeon toes, tied elbows, loaded or bossy shoulders wide on top and straight shoulderblades, flat sides. An exaggerated narrow front not to be enouraged. HEAD AND SKULL — Appleskull, short fore face or down face. EARS — Pricked or tulip. MOUTH — Over or undershot. NECK — Throatiness at the join of neck and jaw, and at base of neck. BODY AND HINDQUARTERS — Short coupled or cramped stance, also an exaggerated arch, a Camel or Humped back (the arch started behind the shoulder-blades), a too short or overlong loin. Straight stifles, poor muscular development of thighs and second thighs. FEET — Splayed, flat or open. TAIL — Gay, ringed or twisted, short or docked. COAT — Wire or Broken coated; a coarse or wooly coat; coarse thick skin.

Note. — Male animals should have two apparently normal testicles fully descended into the scrotum.

MAIN AMERICAN KENNEL CLUB VARIATION TO THE STANDARD FOR WHIPPET —

Size. — Ideal height for dogs, 19 to 22 inches; for bitches, 18 to 21 inches.

WHIPPET REGISTRATIONS 1981 — 87 INCLUSIVE

1981 — 1417
1982 — 1247
1983 — 1295
1984 — 1124
1985 — 1293
1986 — 1172
1987 — 1221

YET TO WIN CRUFTS BEST-IN-SHOW.